P9-CRW-090

POCKET PUZZLES
BRAINTRAINING

ARCTURUS

ARCTURUS

This edition published in 2015 by Arcturus Publishing Limited
26/27 Bickels Yard, 151–153 Bermondsey Street,
London SE1 3HA

Copyright © Arcturus Holdings Limited
Puzzles copyright © Puzzle Press Ltd

All rights reserved. No part of this publication may be reproduced,
stored in a retrieval system, or transmitted, in any form or by any means,
electronic, mechanical, photocopying, recording or otherwise, without
prior written permission in accordance with the provisions of the
Copyright Act 1956 (as amended). Any person or persons who do any
unauthorised act in relation to this publication may be liable to criminal
prosecution and civil claims for damages.

ISBN: 978-1-78599-161-5
AD004939NT

Printed in China

Contents

Domino Placement

A standard set of 28 dominoes has been laid out as shown.

Can you draw in the edges of them all? The check-box is provided as an aid, so that you can see which dominoes have been located.

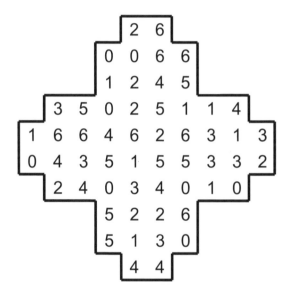

0-0	0-1	0-2	0-3	0-4	0-5	0-6	1-1	1-2	1-3	1-4	1-5	1-6	2-2

2-3	2-4	2-5	2-6	3-3	3-4	3-5	3-6	4-4	4-5	4-6	5-5	5-6	6-6

Hexagony

Can you place the hexagons into the grid, so that where any hexagon touches another along a straight line, the contents of both triangles is the same? No rotation of any hexagon is allowed!

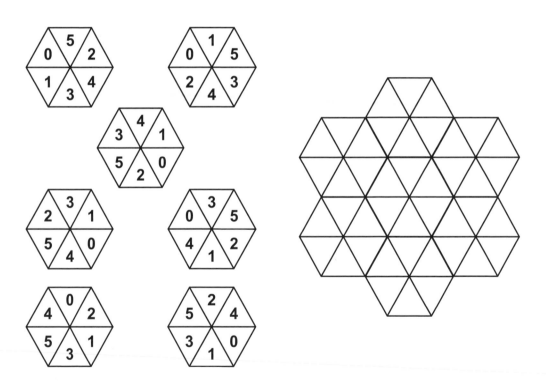

3   Simple as A, B, C?

Each of the small squares in the grid below contains either A, B or C. Every row, column and each of the two long diagonals has exactly two of each letter. The information in the clues refers only to the squares in that row or column. To help you solve this problem, we have provided as many clues as we think you will need! Can you tell the letter in each square?

Across

1 Any three adjacent squares contain three different letters.

2 The As are further right than the Bs.

3 The Bs are next to one another.

4 No two adjacent squares contain the same letter.

5 The Cs are somewhere between the As.

6 The Bs are somewhere between the As.

Down

1 The Cs are lower than the As.

2 Each B is next to and below a C.

3 The As are somewhere between the Bs.

4 The Cs are somewhere between the Bs.

5 Each A is next to and below a B.

6 The Cs are next to and below the As.

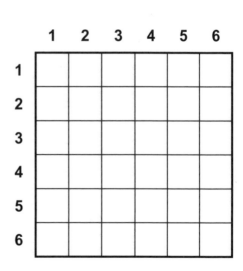

4 Total Concentration

The blank squares below should be filled with whole numbers between 1 and 40 inclusive, any of which may occur more than once, or not at all.

The numbers in every horizontal row add up to the totals on the right, as do the two long diagonal lines; whilst those in every vertical column add up to the totals along the bottom.

Can you discover the missing numbers?

								184
1	24		36	10	9	16	10	139
39		22	2	5		16	13	134
11		18	14	8	26	17	24	125
		14		28	9	37	39	201
	3	31	38	37	5	21		146
20	4		1	5	32			127
12	27	18	15	14	1		18	113
32		35	14			20	14	200
141	137	178	155	146	111	159	158	167

5   Shape Up

Every row and column in this grid originally contained one circle, one diamond, one square, one triangle and two blank squares, although not necessarily in that order.

Every symbol with a black arrow refers to the first of the four symbols encountered when travelling in the direction of the arrow. Every symbol with a white arrow refers to the second of the four symbols encountered in the direction of the arrow.

Can you complete the original grid?

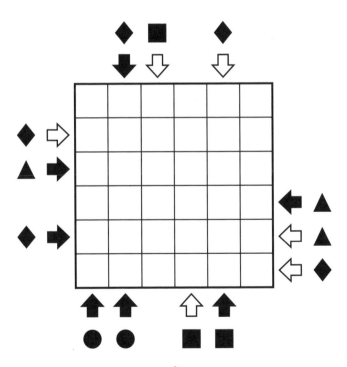

Mind Over Matter

Given that the letters are valued 1-26 according to their places in the alphabet, can you crack the mystery code to reveal the missing letter?

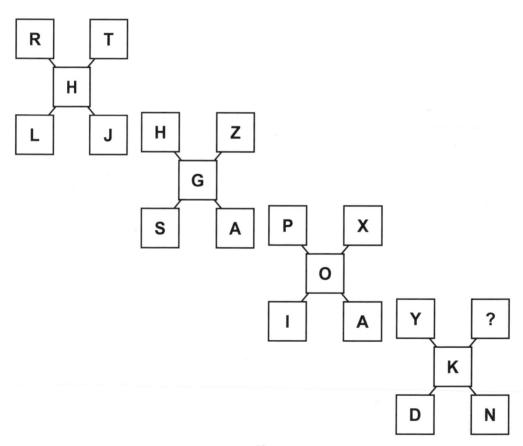

7　　　　　　　　　　　　　**Whatever Next?**

Which of the four lettered alternatives (A, B, C or D) fits most logically into the empty square?

9	2	1
8	3	4
7	6	5

8	1	9
7	2	3
6	5	4

7	9	8
6	1	2
5	4	3

9	8	6
5	1	7
2	3	4

A

1	8	7
6	9	5
4	3	2

B

6	8	7
5	9	1
4	3	2

C

1	8	6
5	9	7
4	2	3

D

8   **The Bottom Line**

Can you fill each square in the bottom line with the correct digit?

Every square in the solution contains only one digit from each of the lettered lines above, although two or more squares in the solution may contain the same digit.

At the end of every row is a score, which shows:

a the number of digits placed in the correct finishing position on the bottom line, as indicated by a tick; and

b the number of digits which appear on the bottom line, but in a different position, as indicated by a cross.

SCORE

2	4	5	0	✓✓
1	1	7	5	✗
0	1	7	3	✗✗✗
4	3	5	6	✓
6	3	7	7	✓
				✓✓✓✓

Combiku

Each horizontal row and vertical column should contain five different shapes and five different numbers.

Every square will contain one number and one shape and no combination may be repeated anywhere else in the puzzle; so, for instance, if a square contains a 3 and a star, then no other square containing a 3 will also contain a star and no other square with a star will contain a 3.

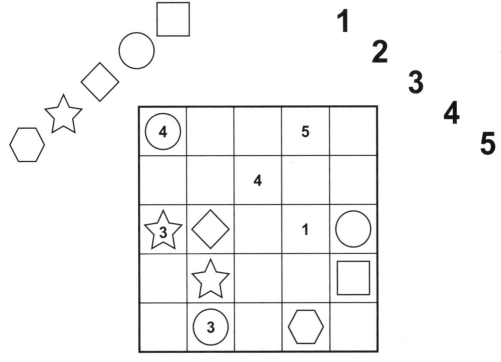

Ls in Place

Twelve L-shapes like the ones here need to be inserted in the grid and each L has one hole in it.

There are three pieces of each of the four kinds shown here and any piece may be turned or flipped over before being put in the grid. No pieces of the same kind may touch, even at a corner.

The pieces fit together so well that you cannot see any spaces between them; only the holes show. Can you tell where the Ls are?

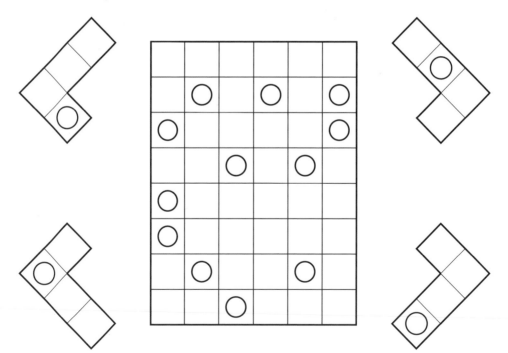

Box Clever

When the box below is folded to form a cube, just one of the five alternatives (A, B, C, D or E) can be produced. Which?

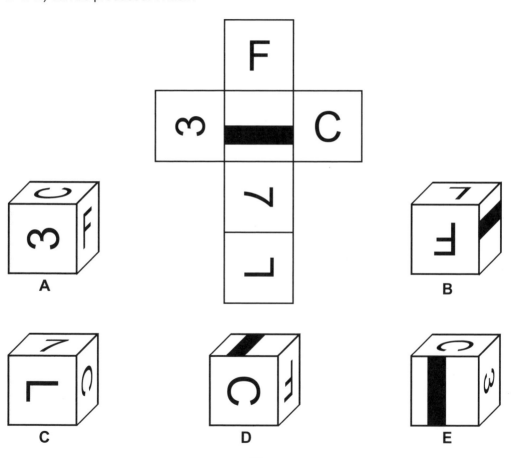

A

B

C

D

E

12   Latin Square

The grid should be filled with numbers from 1 to 6, so that each number appears just once in every row and column. The clues refer to the digit totals in the squares, for example A 1 2 3 = 6 means that the numbers in squares A1, A2 and A3 add up to 6.

1 E 1 2 3 = 11

2 F 3 4 5 = 13

3 C D 1 = 9

4 A B 2 = 11

5 C D 3 = 11

6 C D 4 = 3

7 D E 5 = 8

8 D E 6 = 6

9 A 5 6 = 5

10 B 3 4 = 10

11 C 5 6 = 7

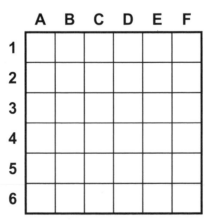

Eliminator

Every oval shape in this diagram contains a different letter of the alphabet from A to K inclusive. Use the clues to determine their locations. Reference in the clues to 'due' means in any location along the same horizontal or vertical line.

1 The A is next to and south of the H, which is next to and west of the E.

2 The B is next to and north of the C, which is next to and east of the F.

3 The D is next to and east of the G, which is next to and north of the K.

4 The I is next to and north of the D, which is due north of (but not next to) the H.

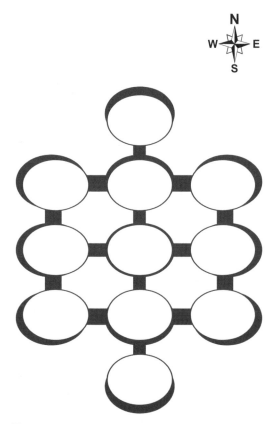

Battleships

Can you place the vessels into the diagram? Some parts of vessels or sea squares
have already been filled in. A number to the right or below a row or column refers to
the number of occupied squares in that row or column. Any vessel may be positioned
horizontally or vertically, but no part of a vessel touches part of any other vessel, either
horizontally, vertically or diagonally.

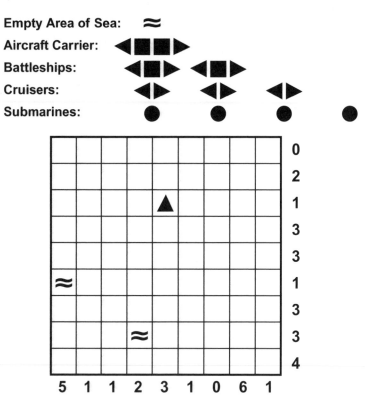

Coin Collecting

In this puzzle, an amateur coin collector has been out with his metal detector, searching for booty. He didn't have time to dig up all the coins he found, so has made a grid map, showing their locations, in the hope that if he loses the map, at least no-one else will understand it... However, he didn't count on YOU coming across the strange grid (as seen here). Will you be able to discover the correct number of coins and their precise locations?

Those squares containing numbers are empty, but where a number appears in a square, it indicates how many coins are located in the squares (up to a maximum of eight) surrounding the numbered one, touching it at any corner or side. There is only one coin in any individual square. Place a circle into every square containing a coin.

	3		1						1
2				1	2		3	2	1
	1			1					
1		1			1			4	1
	1		2			2		4	
						2	4		3
	0				4				
		2						4	3
	3			1		2			
1	3					1	2	3	

Slitherlink

Draw a single continuous loop, by connecting the dots. No line may cross the path of another.

The figure inside each set of any four surrounding dots indicates the total number of surrounding lines.

```
. . . . . . . . . . . .
  2     1  1  1        2
. . . . . . . . . . . .
  1                 3     2        0
. . . . . . . . . . . .
        1  1  1        2  3
. . . . . . . . . . . .
        2  2  2           1
. . . . . . . . . . . .
  1     3  2              1  3
. . . . . . . . . . . .
     1     2  1  3        0  2
. . . . . . . . . . . .
  3     0                 1  1
. . . . . . . . . . . .
        1  3              2  3
. . . . . . . . . . . .
  1                    2  1
. . . . . . . . . . . .
  1  0  1     1     2        2
. . . . . . . . . . . .
  2  2     3     2     3     1
. . . . . . . . . . . .
                       2
. . . . . . . . . . . .
```

Logi-6

Every row and column of this grid should contain one each of the letters A, B, C, D, E and F.

In addition, each of the six shapes (marked by thicker lines) should also contain one each of the letters A, B, C, D, E and F.

Can you complete the grid?

18   Piecework

Place all twelve of the pieces into the grid. Any may be rotated or flipped over, but none may touch another, not even diagonally. The numbers outside the grid refer to the number of consecutive black squares; and each block is separated from the others by at least one white square. For instance, '3 2' could refer to a row with none, one or more white squares, then three black squares, then at least one white square, then two more black squares, followed by any number of white squares.

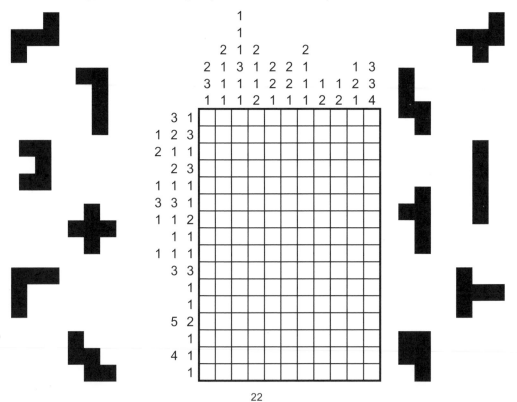

Tile Twister

Place the eight tiles into the puzzle grid so that all adjacent numbers on each tile match up. Tiles may be rotated through 360 degrees, but none may be flipped over.

				2	**2**
				2	**3**

2	**4**
1	**2**

3	**2**
1	**3**

4	**3**
1	**2**

4	**1**
2	**2**

4	**1**
4	**2**

2	**3**
1	**2**

2	**2**
2	**4**

4	**2**
4	**3**

Spot Numbers

The numbers at the top and on the left side show the quantity of single-digit numbers (1-9) used in that row and column. The numbers at the bottom and on the right show the sum of the digits. A number may appear more than once in a row or column, but no numbers are in squares that touch, even at a corner.

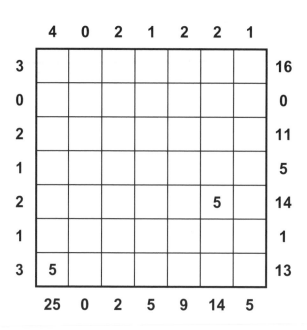

	4	**0**	**2**	**1**	**2**	**2**	**1**	
3								16
0								0
2								11
1								5
2						5		14
1								1
3	5							13
	25	0	2	5	9	14	5	

Domino Placement

A standard set of 28 dominoes has been laid out as shown.

Can you draw in the edges of them all? The check-box is provided as an aid, so that you can see which dominoes have been located.

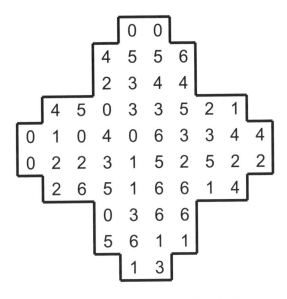

0-0	0-1	0-2	0-3	0-4	0-5	0-6	1-1	1-2	1-3	1-4	1-5	1-6	2-2

2-3	2-4	2-5	2-6	3-3	3-4	3-5	3-6	4-4	4-5	4-6	5-5	5-6	6-6

Hexagony

Can you place the hexagons into the grid, so that where any hexagon touches another along a straight line, the contents of both triangles is the same? No rotation of any hexagon is allowed!

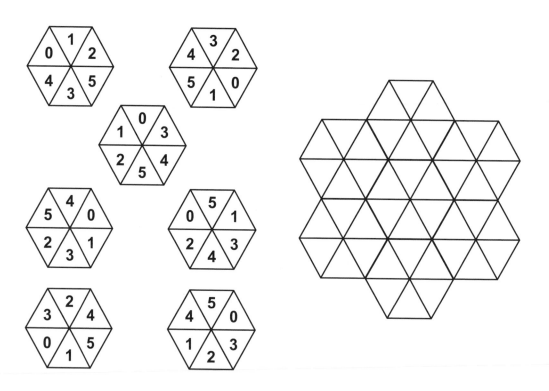

Simple as A, B, C?

Each of the small squares in the grid below contains either A, B or C. Every row, column and each of the two long diagonals has exactly two of each letter. The information in the clues refers only to the squares in that row or column. To help you solve this problem, we have provided as many clues as we think you will need! Can you tell the letter in each square?

Across

1 The As are further right than the Bs.

3 Each C is next to and right of an A.

4 No two adjacent squares contain the same letter.

6 The As are somewhere between the Cs.

Down

3 The Bs are somewhere between the As.

4 The Bs are next to one another.

5 No two adjacent squares contain the same letter.

6 The Bs are lower than the As.

	1	2	3	4	5	6
1						
2						
3						
4						
5						
6						

24   Total Concentration

The blank squares below should be filled with whole numbers between 1 and 40 inclusive, any of which may occur more than once, or not at all.

The numbers in every horizontal row add up to the totals on the right, as do the two long diagonal lines; whilst those in every vertical column add up to the totals along the bottom.

Can you discover the missing numbers?

								241
11	21	29	27		12	24		159
13			1	39	29		21	166
19	9	36	10	8	12		15	119
40	4	9		35	40	14	18	183
33	36		34	37		24	19	237
		37				27	9	188
31	37	16	28	31		33	5	197
19	38	21		14	17	7	34	153
203	**194**	**182**	**154**	**169**	**173**	**175**	**152**	**208**

Shape Up

Every row and column in this grid originally contained one circle, one diamond, one square, one triangle and two blank squares, although not necessarily in that order.

Every symbol with a black arrow refers to the first of the four symbols encountered when travelling in the direction of the arrow. Every symbol with a white arrow refers to the second of the four symbols encountered in the direction of the arrow.

Can you complete the original grid?

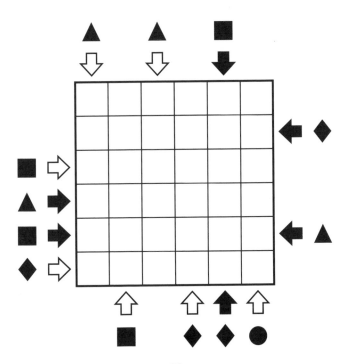

Mind Over Matter

Given that the letters are valued 1-26 according to their places in the alphabet, can you crack the mystery code to reveal the missing letter?

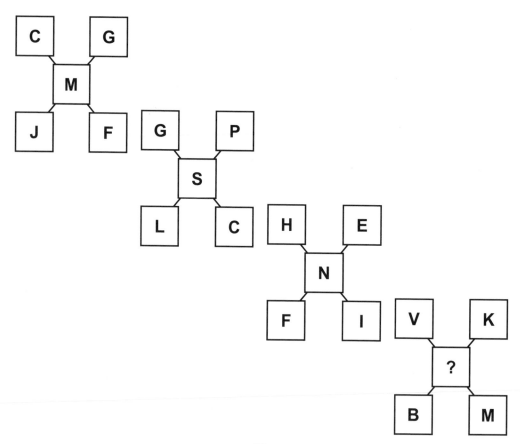

Whatever Next?

Which of the four lettered alternatives (A, B, C or D) fits most logically into the empty square?

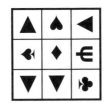

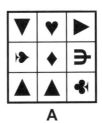
A

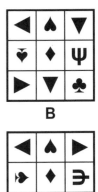
B

C

D

28   The Bottom Line

Can you fill each square in the bottom line with the correct digit?

Every square in the solution contains only one digit from each of the lettered lines above, although two or more squares in the solution may contain the same digit.

At the end of every row is a score, which shows:

a the number of digits placed in the correct finishing position on the bottom line, as indicated by a tick; and

b the number of digits which appear on the bottom line, but in a different position, as indicated by a cross.

SCORE

5	4	1	3	✓ ✗
4	2	7	0	✓ ✗
1	5	0	6	✓
3	1	4	2	✗
0	5	1	3	✓
				✓✓✓✓

Combiku

Each horizontal row and vertical column should contain five different shapes and five different numbers.

Every square will contain one number and one shape and no combination may be repeated anywhere else in the puzzle; so, for instance, if a square contains a 3 and a star, then no other square containing a 3 will also contain a star and no other square with a star will contain a 3.

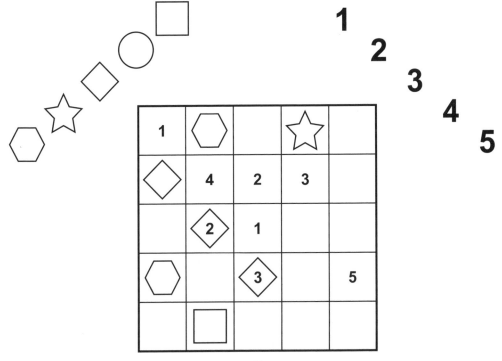

Ls in Place

Twelve L-shapes like the ones here need to be inserted in the grid and each L has one hole in it.

There are three pieces of each of the four kinds shown here and any piece may be turned or flipped over before being put in the grid. No pieces of the same kind may touch, even at a corner.

The pieces fit together so well that you cannot see any spaces between them; only the holes show. Can you tell where the Ls are?

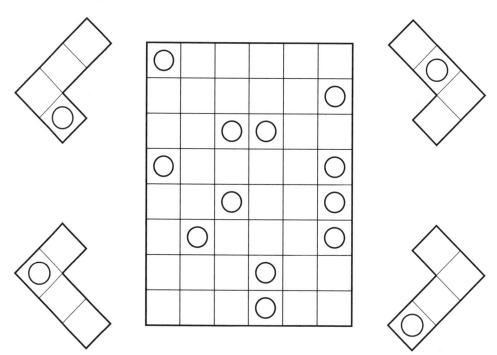

Box Clever

When the box below is folded to form a cube, just one of the five alternatives (A, B, C, D or E) can be produced. Which?

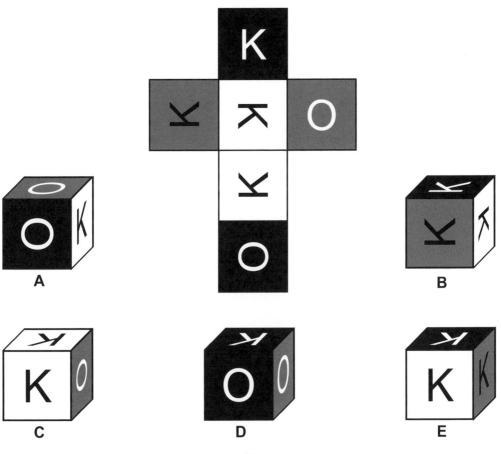

Latin Square

The grid should be filled with numbers from 1 to 6, so that each number appears just once in every row and column. The clues refer to the digit totals in the squares, for example A 1 2 3 = 6 means that the numbers in squares A1, A2 and A3 add up to 6.

1 B C D 4 = 10   **7** D 1 2 = 11

2 D E F 5 = 10   **8** E 2 3 = 11

3 E F 6 = 9   **9** F 1 2 = 3

4 A 5 6 = 6   **10** A B 1 = 4

5 B 5 6 = 11   **11** A B 2 = 5

6 C 5 6 = 5

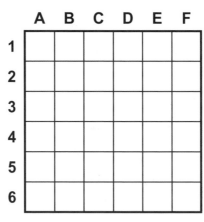

Eliminator

Every oval shape in this diagram contains a different letter of the alphabet from A to K inclusive. Use the clues to determine their locations. Reference in the clues to 'due' means in any location along the same horizontal or vertical line.

1 The A is next to and north of the H, which is next to and east of the J.

2 The B is next to and west of the I, which is next to and north of the K.

3 The C is next to and west of the D, which is further north than the J.

4 The E is further south than the F, but further north than the G (which is further north than the K).

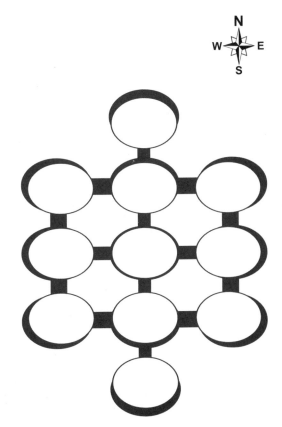

Battleships

Can you place the vessels into the diagram? Some parts of vessels or sea squares have already been filled in. A number to the right or below a row or column refers to the number of occupied squares in that row or column. Any vessel may be positioned horizontally or vertically, but no part of a vessel touches part of any other vessel, either horizontally, vertically or diagonally.

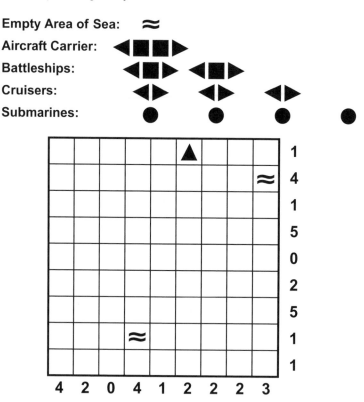

Coin Collecting

In this puzzle, an amateur coin collector has been out with his metal detector, searching for booty. He didn't have time to dig up all the coins he found, so has made a grid map, showing their locations, in the hope that if he loses the map, at least no-one else will understand it... However, he didn't count on YOU coming across the strange grid (as seen here). Will you be able to discover the correct number of coins and their precise locations?

Those squares containing numbers are empty, but where a number appears in a square, it indicates how many coins are located in the squares (up to a maximum of eight) surrounding the numbered one, touching it at any corner or side. There is only one coin in any individual square. Place a circle into every square containing a coin.

		1	2			2		1	
2				4					
							1		0
	1	1		0			2		2
0		1		1		3			
1			3	2			4	3	
1		3	2		2				2
		2			1			2	1
	2						2		

Slitherlink

Draw a single continuous loop, by connecting the dots. No line may cross the path of another.

The figure inside each set of any four surrounding dots indicates the total number of surrounding lines.

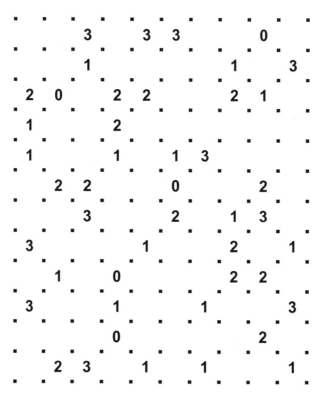

Logi-6

Every row and column of this grid should contain one each of the letters A, B, C, D, E and F.

In addition, each of the six shapes (marked by thicker lines) should also contain one each of the letters A, B, C, D, E and F.

Can you complete the grid?

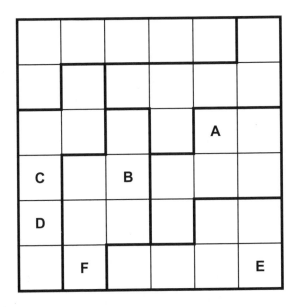

Piecework

Place all twelve of the pieces into the grid. Any may be rotated or flipped over, but none may touch another, not even diagonally. The numbers outside the grid refer to the number of consecutive black squares; and each block is separated from the others by at least one white square. For instance, '3 2' could refer to a row with none, one or more white squares, then three black squares, then at least one white square, then two more black squares, followed by any number of white squares.

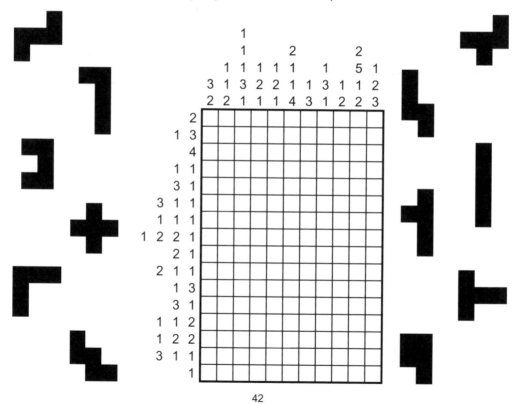

Tile Twister

Place the eight tiles into the puzzle grid so that all adjacent numbers on each tile match up. Tiles may be rotated through 360 degrees, but none may be flipped over.

		4	2		
		3	2		

4	4
1	1

2	2
1	3

4	3
4	2

4	3
2	4

3	1
3	4

2	1
4	3

4	1
3	4

3	1
1	4

Spot Numbers

The numbers at the top and on the left side show the quantity of single-digit numbers (1-9) used in that row and column. The numbers at the bottom and on the right show the sum of the digits. A number may appear more than once in a row or column, but no numbers are in squares that touch, even at a corner.

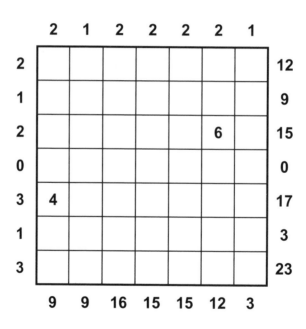

Domino Placement

A standard set of 28 dominoes has been laid out as shown.

Can you draw in the edges of them all? The check-box is provided as an aid, so that you can see which dominoes have been located.

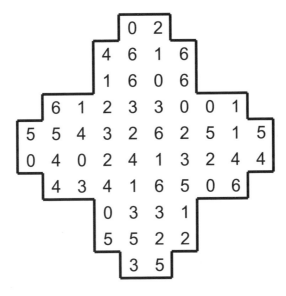

0-0	0-1	0-2	0-3	0-4	0-5	0-6	1-1	1-2	1-3	1-4	1-5	1-6	2-2

2-3	2-4	2-5	2-6	3-3	3-4	3-5	3-6	4-4	4-5	4-6	5-5	5-6	6-6

Hexagony

Can you place the hexagons into the grid, so that where any hexagon touches another along a straight line, the contents of both triangles is the same? No rotation of any hexagon is allowed!

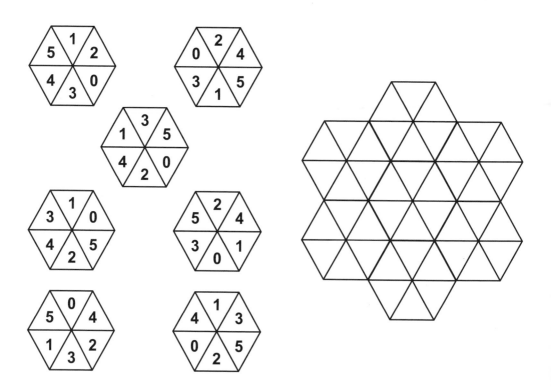

43   Simple as A, B, C?

Each of the small squares in the grid below contains either A, B or C. Every row, column and each of the two long diagonals has exactly two of each letter. The information in the clues refers only to the squares in that row or column. To help you solve this problem, we have provided as many clues as we think you will need! Can you tell the letter in each square?

Across

1. The Bs are next to one another.
2. No two adjacent squares contain the same letter.
3. Any three adjacent squares contain three different letters.
4. Each C is next to and right of a B.
5. The As are somewhere between the Cs.
6. No two adjacent squares contain the same letter.

Down

1. No two adjacent squares contain the same letter.
2. The As are next to one another.
3. The Cs are somewhere between the Bs.
4. The Cs are lower than the As.
5. The Bs are somewhere between the As.
6. The Cs are lower than the As.

	1	2	3	4	5	6
1						
2						
3						
4						
5						
6						

Total Concentration

The blank squares below should be filled with whole numbers between 1 and 40 inclusive, any of which may occur more than once, or not at all.

The numbers in every horizontal row add up to the totals on the right, as do the two long diagonal lines; whilst those in every vertical column add up to the totals along the bottom.

Can you discover the missing numbers?

								149
	35				40		32	**177**
6	6	5	37	34			30	**147**
5	7	34	6		1	28		**112**
10	23	8	31		14	3	8	**98**
34		29		29	35		20	**197**
26	23	35	22		7	26	25	**178**
	28		10	5	9	7	40	**143**
22	31	17		32	12	30	23	**191**
113	**158**	**181**	**147**	**157**	**124**	**179**	**184**	**139**

Shape Up

Every row and column in this grid originally contained one circle, one diamond, one square, one triangle and two blank squares, although not necessarily in that order.

Every symbol with a black arrow refers to the first of the four symbols encountered when travelling in the direction of the arrow. Every symbol with a white arrow refers to the second of the four symbols encountered in the direction of the arrow.

Can you complete the original grid?

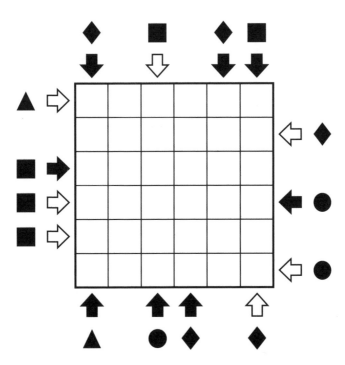

Mind Over Matter

Given that the letters are valued 1-26 according to their places in the alphabet, can you crack the mystery code to reveal the missing letter?

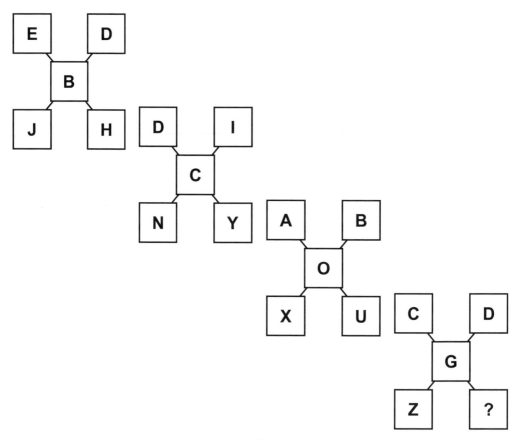

Whatever Next?

Which of the four lettered alternatives (A, B, C or D) fits most logically into the empty square?

A	C	F
P	Y	G
L	M	E

L	A	C
Y	M	F
P	E	G

P	L	A
M	E	C
Y	G	F

M	Y	P
G	F	L
E	C	A

A

Y	P	L
F	G	A
M	E	C

B

M	Y	P
G	C	L
E	F	A

C

Y	P	L
E	G	A
M	F	C

D

The Bottom Line

Can you fill each square in the bottom line with the correct digit?

Every square in the solution contains only one digit from each of the lettered lines above, although two or more squares in the solution may contain the same digit.

At the end of every row is a score, which shows:

a the number of digits placed in the correct finishing position on the bottom line, as indicated by a tick; and

b the number of digits which appear on the bottom line, but in a different position, as indicated by a cross.

SCORE

0	0	6	7	✓
5	1	5	7	✓ ✗
7	0	4	5	✓ ✗
4	0	2	0	✓
2	0	1	3	✓ ✗
				✓✓✓✓

Combiku

Each horizontal row and vertical column should contain five different shapes and five different numbers.

Every square will contain one number and one shape and no combination may be repeated anywhere else in the puzzle; so, for instance, if a square contains a 3 and a star, then no other square containing a 3 will also contain a star and no other square with a star will contain a 3.

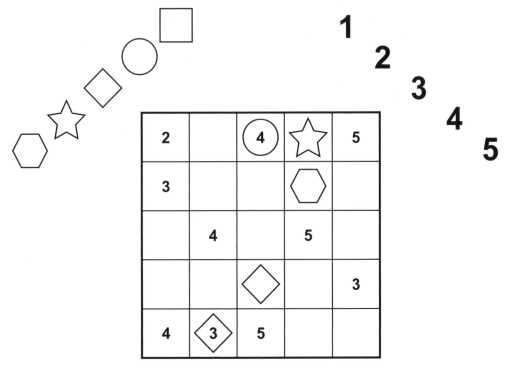

Ls in Place

Twelve L-shapes like the ones here need to be inserted in the grid and each L has one hole in it.

There are three pieces of each of the four kinds shown here and any piece may be turned or flipped over before being put in the grid. No pieces of the same kind may touch, even at a corner.

The pieces fit together so well that you cannot see any spaces between them; only the holes show. Can you tell where the Ls are?

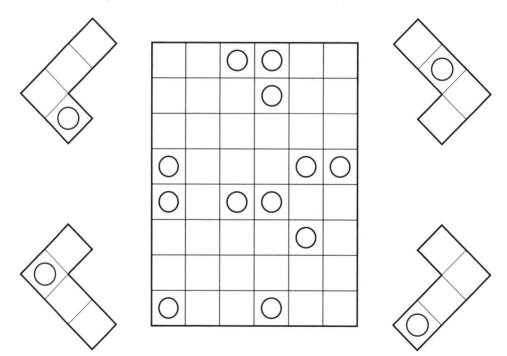

Box Clever

When the box below is folded to form a cube, just one of the five alternatives (A, B, C, D or E) can be produced. Which?

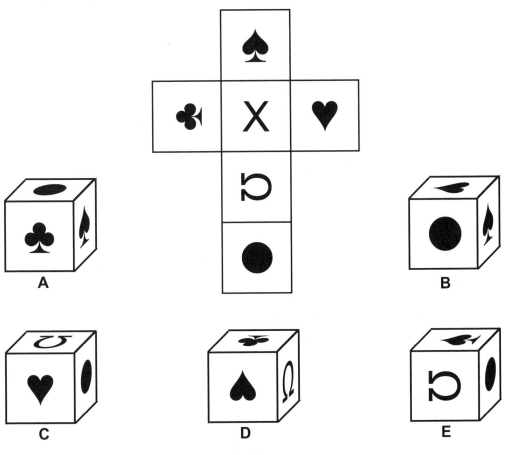

A

B

C

D

E

Latin Square

The grid should be filled with numbers from 1 to 6, so that each number appears just once in every row and column. The clues refer to the digit totals in the squares, for example A 1 2 3 = 6 means that the numbers in squares A1, A2 and A3 add up to 6.

1 C 1 2 3 = 13	**7** A B 3 = 6
2 D 3 4 5 = 14	**8** B C 4 = 5
3 E 5 6 = 6	**9** A B 5 = 7
4 F 2 3 = 5	**10** A B 6 = 9
5 D E 1 = 8	**11** A 1 2 = 10
6 D E 2 = 4	

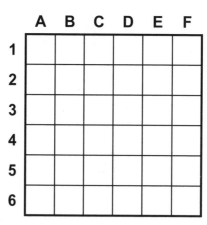

Eliminator

Every oval shape in this diagram contains a different letter of the alphabet from A to K inclusive. Use the clues to determine their locations. Reference in the clues to 'due' means in any location along the same horizontal or vertical line.

1 The A is due south of (but not next to) the C, which is next to and west of the J.

2 The B is next to and north of the I, which is further east than the K.

3 The D is further south than the E and further east than the F.

4 The G is due east of the I, which is due north of the H.

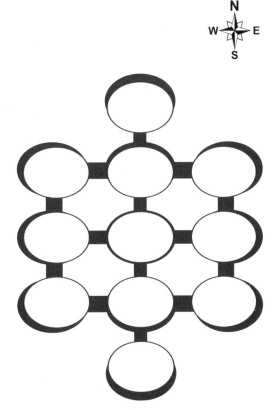

Battleships

Can you place the vessels into the diagram? Some parts of vessels or sea squares have already been filled in. A number to the right or below a row or column refers to the number of occupied squares in that row or column. Any vessel may be positioned horizontally or vertically, but no part of a vessel touches part of any other vessel, either horizontally, vertically or diagonally.

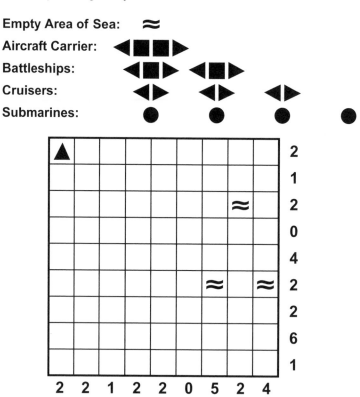

Coin Collecting

In this puzzle, an amateur coin collector has been out with his metal detector, searching for booty. He didn't have time to dig up all the coins he found, so has made a grid map, showing their locations, in the hope that if he loses the map, at least no-one else will understand it... However, he didn't count on YOU coming across the strange grid (as seen here). Will you be able to discover the correct number of coins and their precise locations?

Those squares containing numbers are empty, but where a number appears in a square, it indicates how many coins are located in the squares (up to a maximum of eight) surrounding the numbered one, touching it at any corner or side. There is only one coin in any individual square. Place a circle into every square containing a coin.

2		2				1	1	1
	4		1	1				2
	4		1		0		2	
2			2					
				1		2		2
	4	3						1
						3		1
2					3		3	1
		1						1
2			1	2			3	2

Slitherlink

Draw a single continuous loop, by connecting the dots. No line may cross the path of another.

The figure inside each set of any four surrounding dots indicates the total number of surrounding lines.

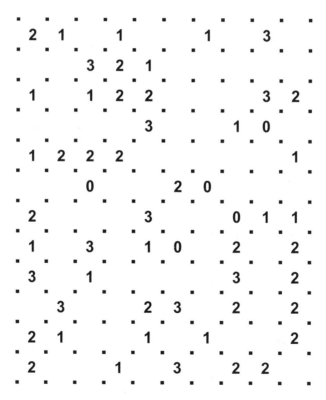

Logi-6

Every row and column of this grid should contain one each of the letters A, B, C, D, E and F.

In addition, each of the six shapes (marked by thicker lines) should also contain one each of the letters A, B, C, D, E and F.

Can you complete the grid?

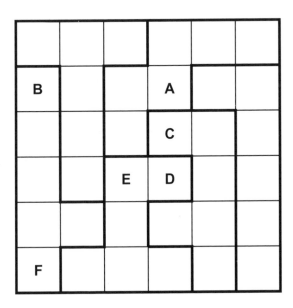

Piecework

Place all twelve of the pieces into the grid. Any may be rotated or flipped over, but none may touch another, not even diagonally. The numbers outside the grid refer to the number of consecutive black squares; and each block is separated from the others by at least one white square. For instance, '3 2' could refer to a row with none, one or more white squares, then three black squares, then at least one white square, then two more black squares, followed by any number of white squares.

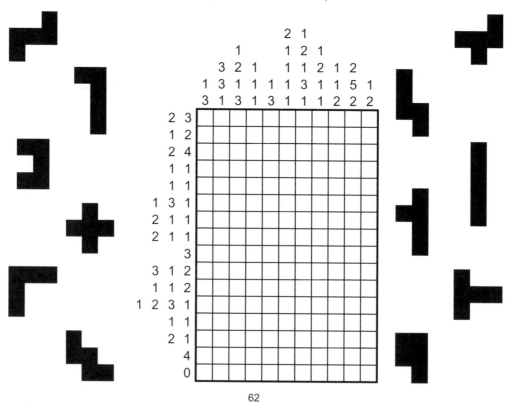

Tile Twister

Place the eight tiles into the puzzle grid so that all adjacent numbers on each tile match up. Tiles may be rotated through 360 degrees, but none may be flipped over.

4	3				
1	1				

3	2
2	4

1	2
2	3

2	2
1	3

1	2
4	4

3	1
3	1

1	3
2	3

3	3
4	2

4	2
4	2

Spot Numbers

The numbers at the top and on the left side show the quantity of single-digit numbers (1-9) used in that row and column. The numbers at the bottom and on the right show the sum of the digits. A number may appear more than once in a row or column, but no numbers are in squares that touch, even at a corner.

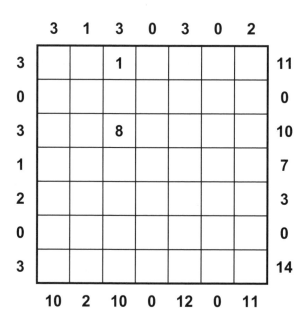

	3	1	3	0	3	0	2	
3			1					11
0								0
3			8					10
1								7
2								3
0								0
3								14
	10	2	10	0	12	0	11	

Domino Placement

A standard set of 28 dominoes has been laid out as shown.

Can you draw in the edges of them all? The check-box is provided as an aid, so that you can see which dominoes have been located.

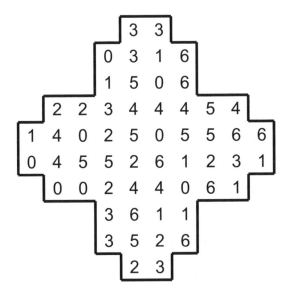

0-0	0-1	0-2	0-3	0-4	0-5	0-6	1-1	1-2	1-3	1-4	1-5	1-6	2-2

2-3	2-4	2-5	2-6	3-3	3-4	3-5	3-6	4-4	4-5	4-6	5-5	5-6	6-6

Hexagony

Can you place the hexagons into the grid, so that where any hexagon touches another along a straight line, the contents of both triangles is the same? No rotation of any hexagon is allowed!

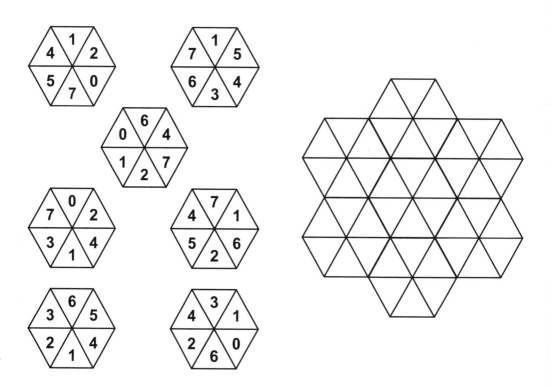

63   Simple as A, B, C?

Each of the small squares in the grid below contains either A, B or C. Every row, column and each of the two long diagonals has exactly two of each letter. The information in the clues refers only to the squares in that row or column. To help you solve this problem, we have provided as many clues as we think you will need! Can you tell the letter in each square?

Across

1 The As are somewhere between the Cs.

2 The Bs are next to one another.

3 No two adjacent squares contain the same letter.

4 The Bs are further right than the As.

5 The As are further right than the Cs.

6 Each C is next to and right of a B.

Down

1 Each A is next to and below a B.

2 No two adjacent squares contain the same letter.

3 The Cs are lower than the Bs.

4 The As are lower than the Cs.

5 Any three adjacent squares contain three different letters.

6 The As are somewhere between the Bs.

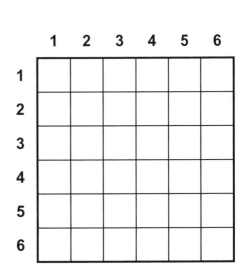

Total Concentration

The blank squares below should be filled with whole numbers between 1 and 40 inclusive, any of which may occur more than once, or not at all.

The numbers in every horizontal row add up to the totals on the right, as do the two long diagonal lines; whilst those in every vertical column add up to the totals along the bottom.

Can you discover the missing numbers?

								129
37	38	7		8	3	10	21	138
13	3	35	40			37	10	177
25	17	5	19		17	11	11	121
11	9	11		2		1	20	94
32		12	21	11	20		6	135
	33		6	18	26		25	150
26	18		39	4		29		150
4		30		22	39	28	38	205
158	157	111	184	105	147	157	151	174

Shape Up

Every row and column in this grid originally contained one circle, one diamond, one square, one triangle and two blank squares, although not necessarily in that order.

Every symbol with a black arrow refers to the first of the four symbols encountered when travelling in the direction of the arrow. Every symbol with a white arrow refers to the second of the four symbols encountered in the direction of the arrow.

Can you complete the original grid?

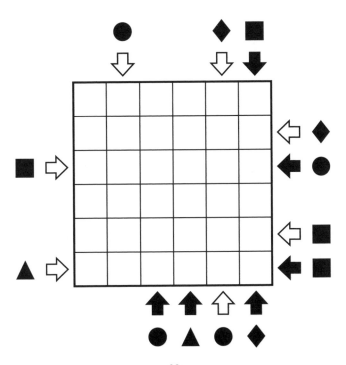

Given that the letters are valued 1-26 according to their places in the alphabet, can you crack the mystery code to reveal the missing letter?

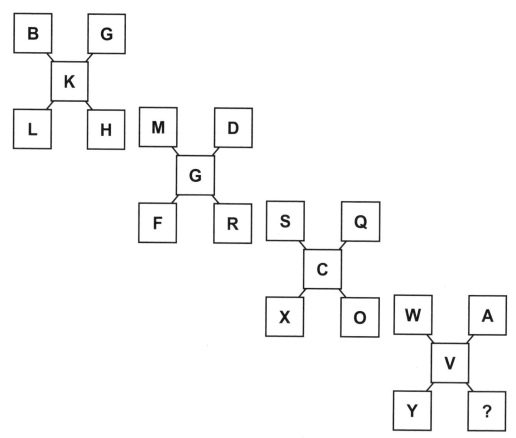

Whatever Next?

Which of the four lettered alternatives (A, B, C or D) fits most logically into the empty square?

A	V	T
I	O	L
W	H	M

ᗺ	Ɱ	∪
ᒐ	ᔮ	Ɯ
✗	⌐	N

Ɔ	X	∧
ꓘ	ᶇ	N
⅄	ſ	O

?

ᗡ	⅄	W
˥	ꓤ	O
Z	ꓘ	ꓒ

A

ᗡ	⅄	Ɯ
˥	ꓤ	O
N	ꓘ	ᔮ

B

ᗡ	ꓤ	Ɯ
˥	⅄	O
N	ꓘ	ᔮ

C

ᗡ	⅄	Ɯ
˥	ꓤ	O
N	ꓘ	ᔮ

D

The Bottom Line

Can you fill each square in the bottom line with the correct digit?

Every square in the solution contains only one digit from each of the lettered lines above, although two or more squares in the solution may contain the same digit.

At the end of every row is a score, which shows:

a the number of digits placed in the correct finishing position on the bottom line, as indicated by a tick; and

b the number of digits which appear on the bottom line, but in a different position, as indicated by a cross.

SCORE

4	0	0	3	✗ ✗
0	4	4	7	✓ ✗
3	4	3	1	✗
1	0	2	6	✗
2	5	6	0	✓ ✓
				✓ ✓ ✓ ✓

Combiku

Each horizontal row and vertical column should contain five different shapes and five different numbers.

Every square will contain one number and one shape and no combination may be repeated anywhere else in the puzzle; so, for instance, if a square contains a 3 and a star, then no other square containing a 3 will also contain a star and no other square with a star will contain a 3.

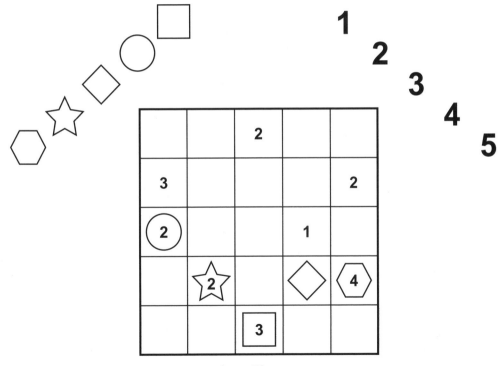

Ls in Place

Twelve L-shapes like the ones here need to be inserted in the grid and each L has one hole in it.

There are three pieces of each of the four kinds shown here and any piece may be turned or flipped over before being put in the grid. No pieces of the same kind may touch, even at a corner.

The pieces fit together so well that you cannot see any spaces between them; only the holes show. Can you tell where the Ls are?

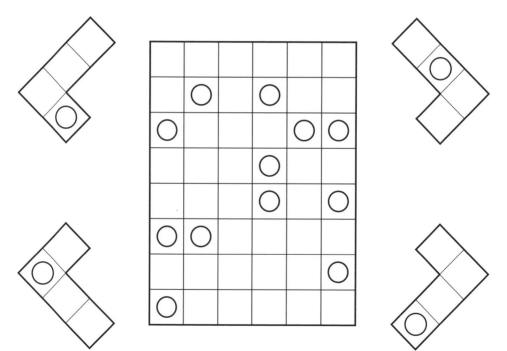

Box Clever

When the box below is folded to form a cube, just one of the five alternatives (A, B, C, D or E) can be produced. Which?

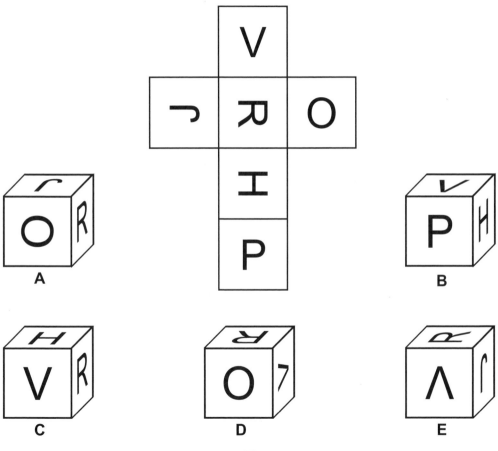

Latin Square

The grid should be filled with numbers from 1 to 6, so that each number appears just once in every row and column. The clues refer to the digit totals in the squares, for example A 1 2 3 = 6 means that the numbers in squares A1, A2 and A3 add up to 6.

1 D 1 2 3 = 6   **7** A B 4 = 10

2 E 3 4 5 = 11   **8** C D 5 = 5

3 F 4 5 = 3   **9** C D 6 = 8

4 E F 1 = 9   **10** A 5 6 = 7

5 E F 2 = 7   **11** B 5 6 = 6

6 A B 3 = 7

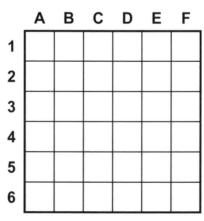

Eliminator

Every oval shape in this diagram contains a different letter of the alphabet from A to K inclusive. Use the clues to determine their locations. Reference in the clues to 'due' means in any location along the same horizontal or vertical line.

1 The A is next to and west of the G, which is due south of the K.

2 The B is further north than the F and further west than the D.

3 The D is next to and north of the H.

4 The I is further north than the J, but further south than the G.

5 The J is next to and east of the C (which is due south of the E).

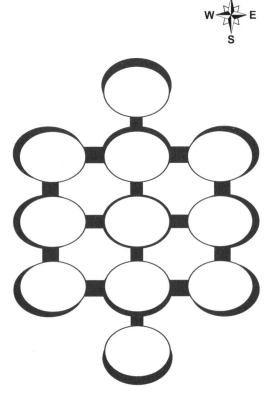

Battleships

Can you place the vessels into the diagram? Some parts of vessels or sea squares have already been filled in. A number to the right or below a row or column refers to the number of occupied squares in that row or column. Any vessel may be positioned horizontally or vertically, but no part of a vessel touches part of any other vessel, either horizontally, vertically or diagonally.

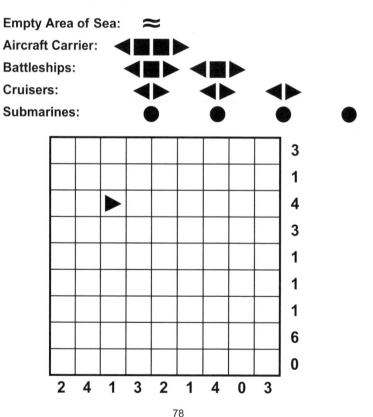

Coin Collecting

In this puzzle, an amateur coin collector has been out with his metal detector, searching for booty. He didn't have time to dig up all the coins he found, so has made a grid map, showing their locations, in the hope that if he loses the map, at least no-one else will understand it... However, he didn't count on YOU coming across the strange grid (as seen here). Will you be able to discover the correct number of coins and their precise locations?

Those squares containing numbers are empty, but where a number appears in a square, it indicates how many coins are located in the squares (up to a maximum of eight) surrounding the numbered one, touching it at any corner or side. There is only one coin in any individual square. Place a circle into every square containing a coin.

		0					2		3
	0				1	1			
		1		1	1	1		3	
0				2		3		4	
	2					4			
		3				5			
	3		1						0
		1		1	3		4	2	
1					3		4		2
			3			1			

Slitherlink

Draw a single continuous loop, by connecting the dots. No line may cross the path of another.

The figure inside each set of any four surrounding dots indicates the total number of surrounding lines.

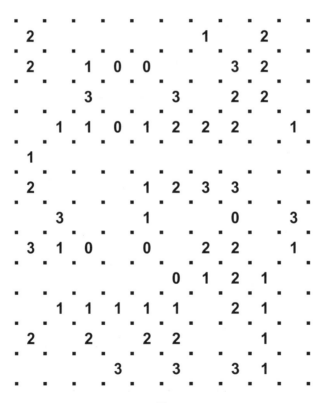

Logi-6

Every row and column of this grid should contain one each of the letters A, B, C, D, E and F.

In addition, each of the six shapes (marked by thicker lines) should also contain one each of the letters A, B, C, D, E and F.

Can you complete the grid?

B		A			
	D		C		
	E				
			F		

Piecework

Place all twelve of the pieces into the grid. Any may be rotated or flipped over, but none may touch another, not even diagonally. The numbers outside the grid refer to the number of consecutive black squares; and each block is separated from the others by at least one white square. For instance, '3 2' could refer to a row with none, one or more white squares, then three black squares, then at least one white square, then two more black squares, followed by any number of white squares.

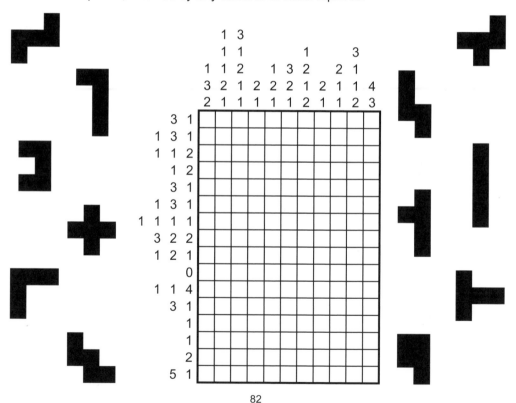

Tile Twister

Place the eight tiles into the puzzle grid so that all adjacent numbers on each tile match up. Tiles may be rotated through 360 degrees, but none may be flipped over.

				3	1
				3	2

4	2
2	3

3	3
1	4

4	4
1	1

1	3
4	2

4	3
3	2

1	1
4	1

4	3
1	2

1	4
3	2

80

Spot Numbers

The numbers at the top and on the left side show the quantity of single-digit numbers (1-9) used in that row and column. The numbers at the bottom and on the right show the sum of the digits. A number may appear more than once in a row or column, but no numbers are in squares that touch, even at a corner.

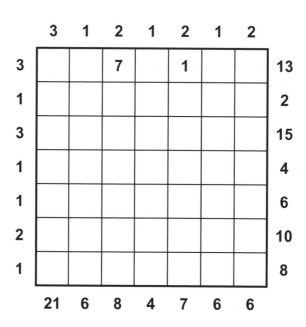

Domino Placement

A standard set of 28 dominoes has been laid out as shown.

Can you draw in the edges of them all? The check-box is provided as an aid, so that you can see which dominoes have been located.

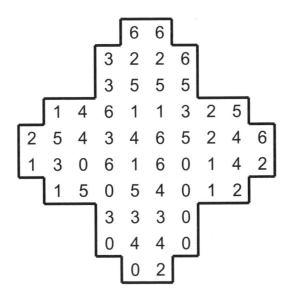

0-0	0-1	0-2	0-3	0-4	0-5	0-6	1-1	1-2	1-3	1-4	1-5	1-6	2-2

2-3	2-4	2-5	2-6	3-3	3-4	3-5	3-6	4-4	4-5	4-6	5-5	5-6	6-6

Hexagony

Can you place the hexagons into the grid, so that where any hexagon touches another along a straight line, the contents of both triangles is the same? No rotation of any hexagon is allowed!

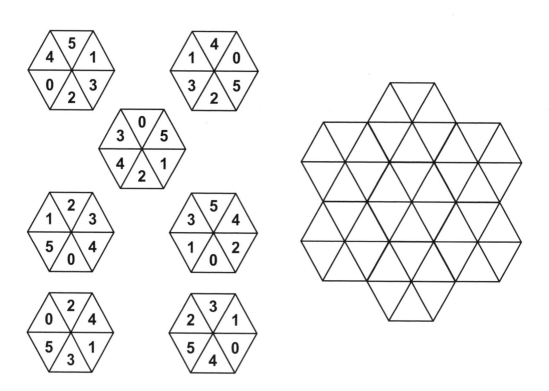

83   Simple as A, B, C?

Each of the small squares in the grid below contains either A, B or C. Every row, column and each of the two long diagonals has exactly two of each letter. The information in the clues refers only to the squares in that row or column. To help you solve this problem, we have provided as many clues as we think you will need! Can you tell the letter in each square?

Across

2 The As are further right than the Bs.

6 The Bs are somewhere between the As.

Down

3 The Cs are somewhere between the As.

4 The Cs are next to one another.

5 Each B is next to and below a C.

84   Total Concentration

The blank squares below should be filled with whole numbers between 1 and 40 inclusive, any of which may occur more than once, or not at all.

The numbers in every horizontal row add up to the totals on the right, as do the two long diagonal lines; whilst those in every vertical column add up to the totals along the bottom.

Can you discover the missing numbers?

								163
18	11	18	20		37	19	7	169
19	34		14	8	28	5	8	150
39		34		5		36	25	243
28	38	7	19	21			36	164
	31		36	38	31	34	19	242
		31	10		5	8		138
28	10	14	3			16	20	127
19	21	38	1	38	6			199
201	205	190	142	188	144	170	192	202

Shape Up

Every row and column in this grid originally contained one circle, one diamond, one square, one triangle and two blank squares, although not necessarily in that order.

Every symbol with a black arrow refers to the first of the four symbols encountered when travelling in the direction of the arrow. Every symbol with a white arrow refers to the second of the four symbols encountered in the direction of the arrow.

Can you complete the original grid?

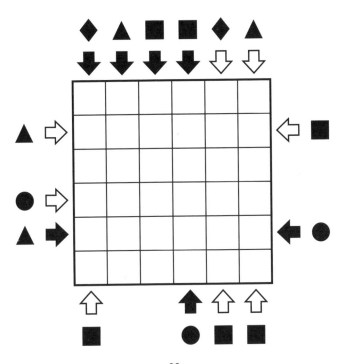

Mind Over Matter

Given that the letters are valued 1-26 according to their places in the alphabet, can you crack the mystery code to reveal the missing letter?

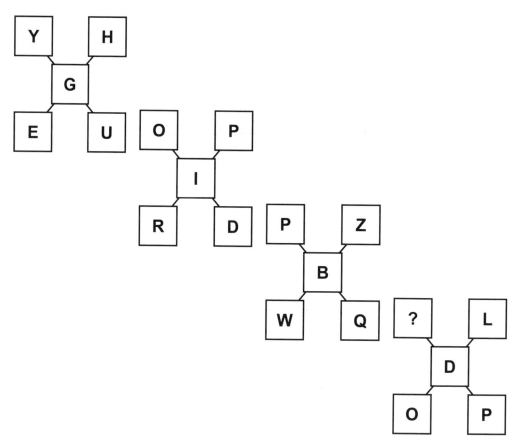

Whatever Next?

Which of the four lettered alternatives (A, B, C or D) fits most logically into the empty square?

8	15	13
15	17	22
7	2	9

4	7	11
5	19	17
1	12	6

5	11	15
17	13	18
12	2	3

13	6	4
20	14	15
7	8	12

A

12	6	3
17	9	18
5	3	16

B

7	14	5
16	20	19
9	6	14

C

5	4	14
19	9	16
13	5	2

D

The Bottom Line

Can you fill each square in the bottom line with the correct digit?

Every square in the solution contains only one digit from each of the lettered lines above, although two or more squares in the solution may contain the same digit.

At the end of every row is a score, which shows:

a the number of digits placed in the correct finishing position on the bottom line, as indicated by a tick; and

b the number of digits which appear on the bottom line, but in a different position, as indicated by a cross.

SCORE

2	2	5	4	✔✔
2	7	3	1	✔✔
5	0	6	4	✘
7	2	5	7	✔✘
3	1	3	3	✔
				✔✔✔✔

Combiku

Each horizontal row and vertical column should contain five different shapes and five different numbers.

Every square will contain one number and one shape and no combination may be repeated anywhere else in the puzzle; so, for instance, if a square contains a 3 and a star, then no other square containing a 3 will also contain a star and no other square with a star will contain a 3.

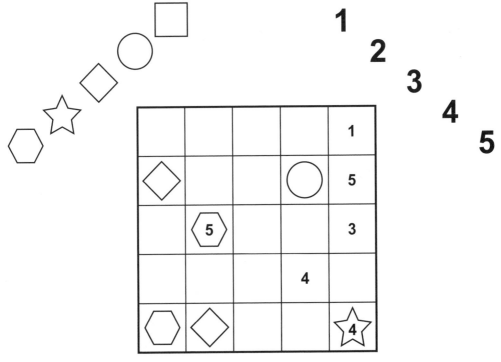

Ls in Place

Twelve L-shapes like the ones here need to be inserted in the grid and each L has one hole in it.

There are three pieces of each of the four kinds shown here and any piece may be turned or flipped over before being put in the grid. No pieces of the same kind may touch, even at a corner.

The pieces fit together so well that you cannot see any spaces between them; only the holes show. Can you tell where the Ls are?

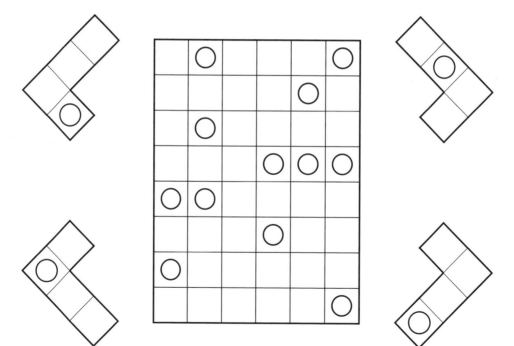

Box Clever

When the box below is folded to form a cube, just one of the five alternatives (A, B, C, D or E) can be produced. Which?

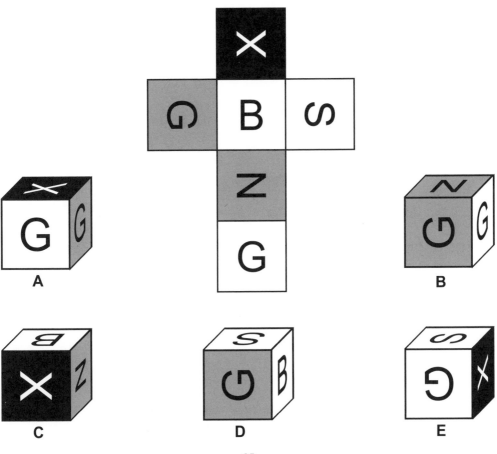

A

B

C

D

E

Latin Square

The grid should be filled with numbers from 1 to 6, so that each number appears just once in every row and column. The clues refer to the digit totals in the squares, for example A 1 2 3 = 6 means that the numbers in squares A1, A2 and A3 add up to 6.

1 D E F 2 = 7   **7** B 2 3 = 4

2 E F 3 = 11   **8** C 1 2 = 6

3 B C 4 = 9   **9** D 3 4 = 10

4 B C 5 = 5   **10** E 4 5 = 8

5 C D E 6 = 10   **11** F 4 5 = 8

6 A 2 3 = 9

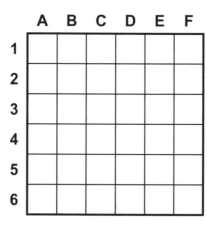

Eliminator

Every oval shape in this diagram contains a different letter of the alphabet from A to K inclusive. Use the clues to determine their locations. Reference in the clues to 'due' means in any location along the same horizontal or vertical line.

1 The A is next to and south of the K, which is next to and east of the C.

2 The B is next to and north of the I, which is next to and west of the G.

3 The D is due south of both the G and the E.

4 The H is next to and north of the F, which is next to and west of the J, which is further north than the C.

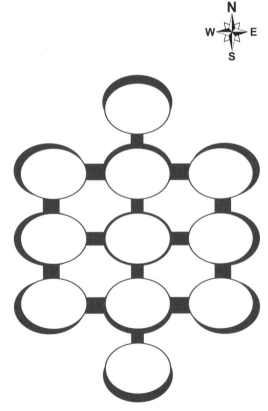

Battleships

Can you place the vessels into the diagram? Some parts of vessels or sea squares have already been filled in. A number to the right or below a row or column refers to the number of occupied squares in that row or column. Any vessel may be positioned horizontally or vertically, but no part of a vessel touches part of any other vessel, either horizontally, vertically or diagonally.

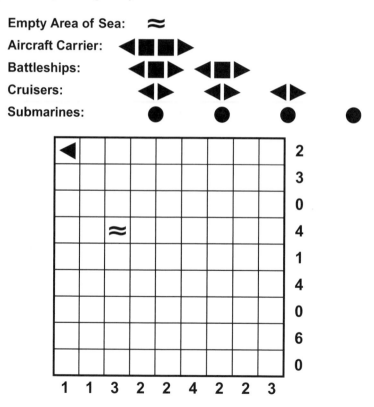

Coin Collecting

In this puzzle, an amateur coin collector has been out with his metal detector, searching for booty. He didn't have time to dig up all the coins he found, so has made a grid map, showing their locations, in the hope that if he loses the map, at least no-one else will understand it... However, he didn't count on YOU coming across the strange grid (as seen here). Will you be able to discover the correct number of coins and their precise locations?

Those squares containing numbers are empty, but where a number appears in a square, it indicates how many coins are located in the squares (up to a maximum of eight) surrounding the numbered one, touching it at any corner or side. There is only one coin in any individual square. Place a circle into every square containing a coin.

1									
		1	1		1		2		2
3			0				1	2	
4			0			0			
				0			2		3
							1	3	
0		2	3		2	2			3
		2				4		4	
1		3	5						1
			3			2	2	2	

Slitherlink

Draw a single continuous loop, by connecting the dots. No line may cross the path of another.

The figure inside each set of any four surrounding dots indicates the total number of surrounding lines.

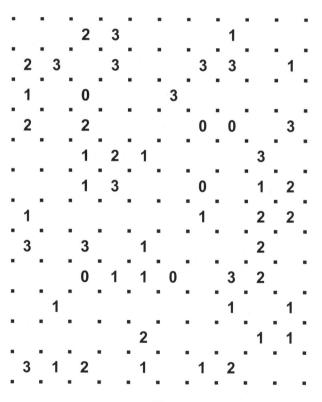

Logi-6

Every row and column of this grid should contain one each of the letters A, B, C, D, E and F.

In addition, each of the six shapes (marked by thicker lines) should also contain one each of the letters A, B, C, D, E and F.

Can you complete the grid?

		B	A		
					C
E				D	
					F

Piecework

Place all twelve of the pieces into the grid. Any may be rotated or flipped over, but none may touch another, not even diagonally. The numbers outside the grid refer to the number of consecutive black squares; and each block is separated from the others by at least one white square. For instance, '3 2' could refer to a row with none, one or more white squares, then three black squares, then at least one white square, then two more black squares, followed by any number of white squares.

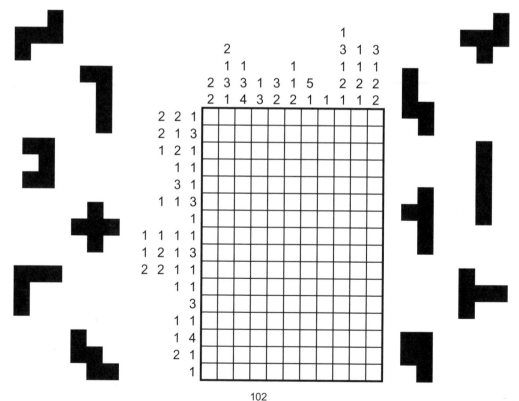

Tile Twister

Place the eight tiles into the puzzle grid so that all adjacent numbers on each tile match up. Tiles may be rotated through 360 degrees, but none may be flipped over.

				3	2
				4	4

1	2
4	4

3	1
1	2

2	4
3	1

2	1
1	2

4	4
3	1

4	2
4	1

3	1
4	2

1	4
1	2

Spot Numbers

The numbers at the top and on the left side show the quantity of single-digit numbers (1-9) used in that row and column. The numbers at the bottom and on the right show the sum of the digits. A number may appear more than once in a row or column, but no numbers are in squares that touch, even at a corner.

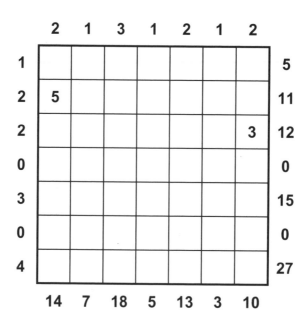

Domino Placement

A standard set of 28 dominoes has been laid out as shown.

Can you draw in the edges of them all? The check-box is provided as an aid, so that you can see which dominoes have been located.

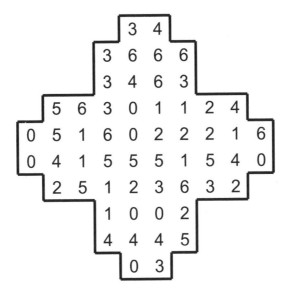

0-0	0-1	0-2	0-3	0-4	0-5	0-6	1-1	1-2	1-3	1-4	1-5	1-6	2-2

2-3	2-4	2-5	2-6	3-3	3-4	3-5	3-6	4-4	4-5	4-6	5-5	5-6	6-6

Hexagony

Can you place the hexagons into the grid, so that where any hexagon touches another along a straight line, the contents of both triangles is the same? No rotation of any hexagon is allowed!

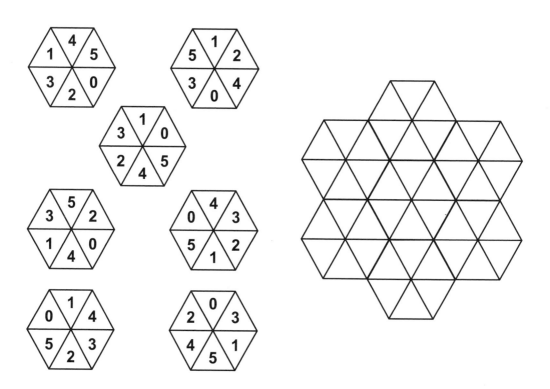

Simple as A, B, C?

Each of the small squares in the grid below contains either A, B or C. Every row, column and each of the two long diagonals has exactly two of each letter. The information in the clues refers only to the squares in that row or column. To help you solve this problem, we have provided as many clues as we think you will need! Can you tell the letter in each square?

Across

1 The Cs are somewhere between the Bs.

2 The Bs are further right than the Cs.

6 Each A is next to and right of a B.

Down

1 The Cs are lower than the Bs.

2 The Bs are lower than the As.

5 The Cs are lower than the Bs.

6 The Cs are lower than the Bs.

	1	2	3	4	5	6
1						
2						
3						
4						
5						
6						

Total Concentration

The blank squares below should be filled with whole numbers between 1 and 40 inclusive, any of which may occur more than once, or not at all.

The numbers in every horizontal row add up to the totals on the right, as do the two long diagonal lines; whilst those in every vertical column add up to the totals along the bottom.

Can you discover the missing numbers?

								245
31	15		15		7	28	17	168
	6	13		12	18			170
22	2	15		14	39	17	17	135
38	39		39	23		8	2	187
	2	14	23		3	1	11	80
32	8	38		12	7	40	5	147
3		11	27	29		38		192
	38	8	35	16	38	35	10	215
193	**146**	**145**	**191**	**139**	**179**	**201**	**100**	**162**

Shape Up

Every row and column in this grid originally contained one circle, one diamond, one square, one triangle and two blank squares, although not necessarily in that order.

Every symbol with a black arrow refers to the first of the four symbols encountered when travelling in the direction of the arrow. Every symbol with a white arrow refers to the second of the four symbols encountered in the direction of the arrow.

Can you complete the original grid?

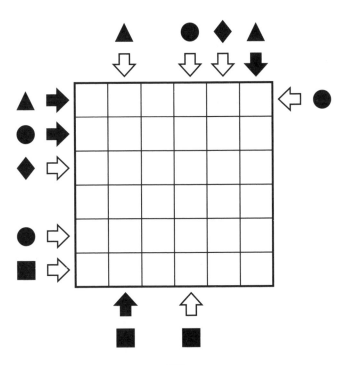

Mind Over Matter

Given that the letters are valued 1-26 according to their places in the alphabet, can you crack the mystery code to reveal the missing letter?

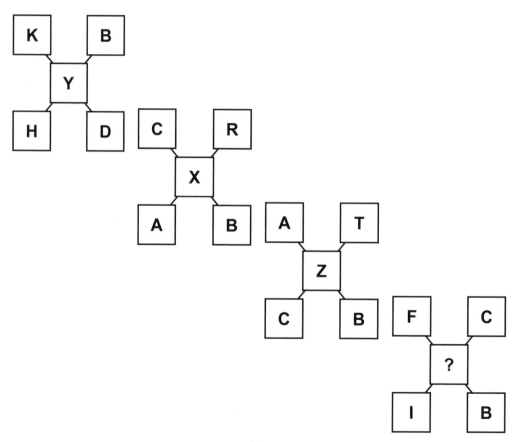

Which of the four lettered alternatives (A, B, C or D) fits most logically into the empty square?

6	16	9
12	5	3
5	3	13

8	6	8
4	10	10
11	8	7

5	7	1
9	14	18
9	3	6

?

16	1	7
3	15	6
4	8	9

A

10	12	3
3	9	14
10	3	8

B

7	14	5
9	5	7
7	5	12

C

17	10	8
2	13	7
4	2	11

D

The Bottom Line

Can you fill each square in the bottom line with the correct digit?

Every square in the solution contains only one digit from each of the lettered lines above, although two or more squares in the solution may contain the same digit.

At the end of every row is a score, which shows:

a the number of digits placed in the correct finishing position on the bottom line, as indicated by a tick; and

b the number of digits which appear on the bottom line, but in a different position, as indicated by a cross.

SCORE

5	4	5	0	✓ ✗ ✗
7	3	7	1	✗
3	4	0	7	✓ ✗ ✗
1	4	7	3	✗ ✗
6	7	3	0	✓ ✗
				✓ ✓ ✓ ✓

Combiku

Each horizontal row and vertical column should contain five different shapes and five different numbers.

Every square will contain one number and one shape and no combination may be repeated anywhere else in the puzzle; so, for instance, if a square contains a 3 and a star, then no other square containing a 3 will also contain a star and no other square with a star will contain a 3.

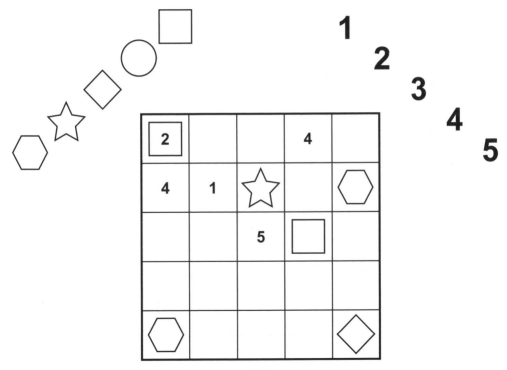

Ls in Place

Twelve L-shapes like the ones here need to be inserted in the grid and each L has one hole in it.

There are three pieces of each of the four kinds shown here and any piece may be turned or flipped over before being put in the grid. No pieces of the same kind may touch, even at a corner.

The pieces fit together so well that you cannot see any spaces between them; only the holes show. Can you tell where the Ls are?

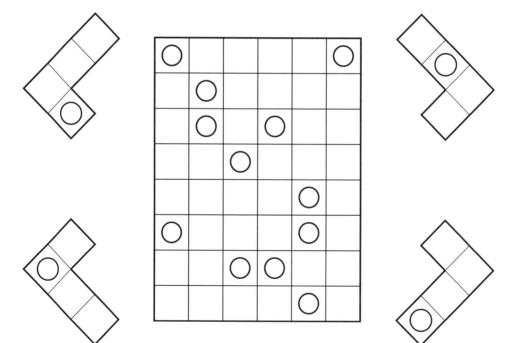

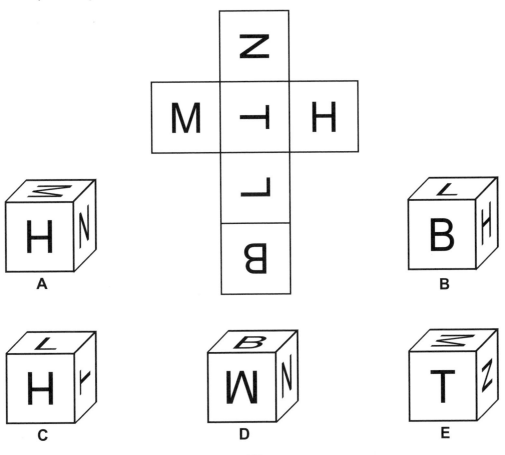

111   Box Clever

When the box below is folded to form a cube, just one of the five alternatives (A, B, C, D or E) can be produced. Which?

A

B

C

D

E

Latin Square

The grid should be filled with numbers from 1 to 6, so that each number appears just once in every row and column. The clues refer to the digit totals in the squares, for example A 1 2 3 = 6 means that the numbers in squares A1, A2 and A3 add up to 6.

1 D E 4 = 11	**7** D 1 2 3 = 7
2 B C 5 = 9	**8** E 5 6 = 8
3 C D 6 = 6	**9** F 3 4 5 = 6
4 A 5 6 = 5	**10** E F 1 = 9
5 B 2 3 = 11	**11** E F 2 = 7
6 C 1 2 = 5	

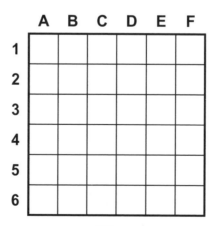

Eliminator

Every oval shape in this diagram contains a different letter of the alphabet from A to K inclusive. Use the clues to determine their locations. Reference in the clues to 'due' means in any location along the same horizontal or vertical line.

1 The A is next to and south of the G, which is next to and south of the C.

2 The B is next to and east of the I, which is due south of the D.

3 The E is next to and north of the K, which is due west of both the C and the F.

4 The J is further east than the H.

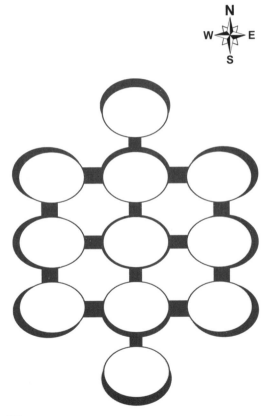

Battleships

Can you place the vessels into the diagram? Some parts of vessels or sea squares have already been filled in. A number to the right or below a row or column refers to the number of occupied squares in that row or column. Any vessel may be positioned horizontally or vertically, but no part of a vessel touches part of any other vessel, either horizontally, vertically or diagonally.

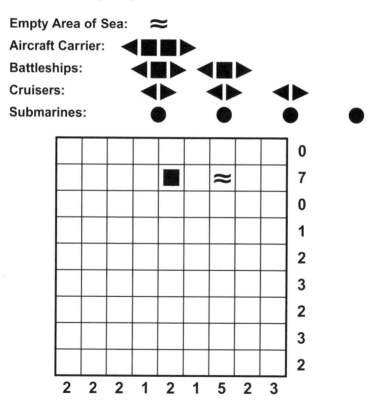

Coin Collecting

In this puzzle, an amateur coin collector has been out with his metal detector, searching for booty. He didn't have time to dig up all the coins he found, so has made a grid map, showing their locations, in the hope that if he loses the map, at least no-one else will understand it... However, he didn't count on YOU coming across the strange grid (as seen here). Will you be able to discover the correct number of coins and their precise locations?

Those squares containing numbers are empty, but where a number appears in a square, it indicates how many coins are located in the squares (up to a maximum of eight) surrounding the numbered one, touching it at any corner or side. There is only one coin in any individual square. Place a circle into every square containing a coin.

1			2		2				2
						1			
		1	1	2	3		3		1
	1	1							0
1		3		3					
				3	3	3	3		
1				2	2				1
3	5					2	3		
			2	2	2				
	3		0					1	

Slitherlink

Draw a single continuous loop, by connecting the dots. No line may cross the path of another.

The figure inside each set of any four surrounding dots indicates the total number of surrounding lines.

Logi-6

Every row and column of this grid should contain one each of the letters A, B, C, D, E and F.

In addition, each of the six shapes (marked by thicker lines) should also contain one each of the letters A, B, C, D, E and F.

Can you complete the grid?

			B	A	
		D	C		
E					
				F	

Piecework

Place all twelve of the pieces into the grid. Any may be rotated or flipped over, but none may touch another, not even diagonally. The numbers outside the grid refer to the number of consecutive black squares; and each block is separated from the others by at least one white square. For instance, '3 2' could refer to a row with none, one or more white squares, then three black squares, then at least one white square, then two more black squares, followed by any number of white squares.

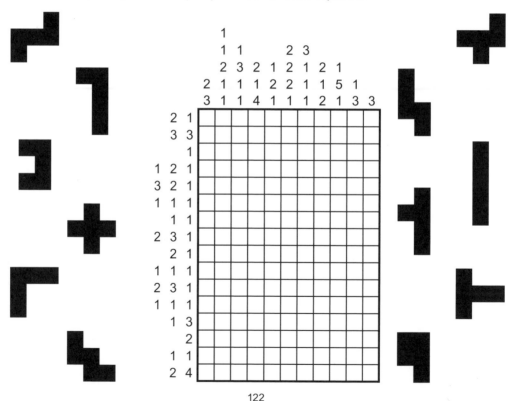

Tile Twister

Place the eight tiles into the puzzle grid so that all adjacent numbers on each tile match up. Tiles may be rotated through 360 degrees, but none may be flipped over.

		1	1		
		1	1		

1	2
2	4

4	1
2	1

3	1
3	1

4	1
3	1

3	3
2	1

4	4
1	2

4	3
1	2

4	4
1	3

Spot Numbers

The numbers at the top and on the left side show the quantity of single-digit numbers (1-9) used in that row and column. The numbers at the bottom and on the right show the sum of the digits. A number may appear more than once in a row or column, but no numbers are in squares that touch, even at a corner.

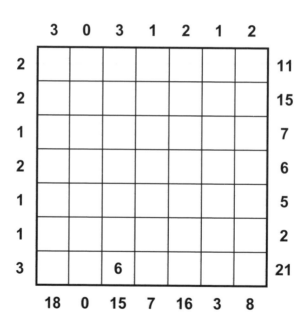

Domino Placement

A standard set of 28 dominoes has been laid out as shown.

Can you draw in the edges of them all? The check-box is provided as an aid, so that you can see which dominoes have been located.

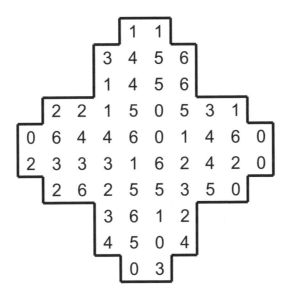

0-0	0-1	0-2	0-3	0-4	0-5	0-6	1-1	1-2	1-3	1-4	1-5	1-6	2-2

2-3	2-4	2-5	2-6	3-3	3-4	3-5	3-6	4-4	4-5	4-6	5-5	5-6	6-6

Hexagony

Can you place the hexagons into the grid, so that where any hexagon touches another along a straight line, the contents of both triangles is the same? No rotation of any hexagon is allowed!

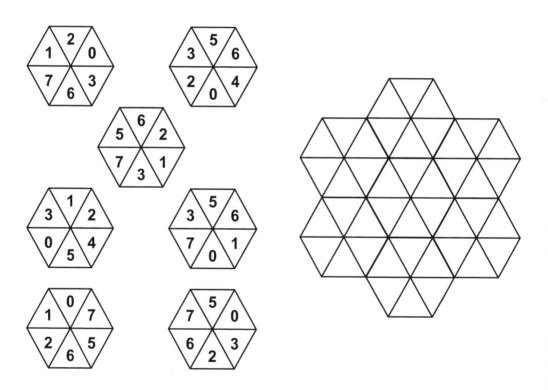

123   Simple as A, B, C?

Each of the small squares in the grid below contains either A, B or C. Every row, column and each of the two long diagonals has exactly two of each letter. The information in the clues refers only to the squares in that row or column. To help you solve this problem, we have provided as many clues as we think you will need! Can you tell the letter in each square?

Across

1 No two adjacent squares contain the same letter.
2 The As are further right than the Bs.
3 Each C is next to and right of a B.
4 Each B is next to and right of an A.
5 The Bs are further right than the As.
6 The Bs are next to one another.

Down

1 Each C is next to and below an A.
2 The Bs are somewhere between the Cs.
3 The Bs are lower than the Cs.
4 The As are next to one another.
5 The As are next to one another.
6 The Cs are somewhere between the Bs.

	1	2	3	4	5	6
1						
2						
3						
4						
5						
6						

Total Concentration

The blank squares below should be filled with whole numbers between 1 and 40 inclusive, any of which may occur more than once, or not at all.

The numbers in every horizontal row add up to the totals on the right, as do the two long diagonal lines; whilst those in every vertical column add up to the totals along the bottom.

Can you discover the missing numbers?

								112
21	3	24		5	38		7	**145**
3	14	10	30	19	8	12		**108**
12			26		2		24	**140**
	36	29	18		37	4	35	**189**
	18	25	2	25		6		**143**
	14	13	34			38	34	**220**
27	39	3	21	9	34	18		**186**
14	16	19	19		4	21	15	**117**
136	**147**	**141**	**175**	**140**	**157**	**154**	**198**	**147**

Shape Up

Every row and column in this grid originally contained one circle, one diamond, one square, one triangle and two blank squares, although not necessarily in that order.

Every symbol with a black arrow refers to the first of the four symbols encountered when travelling in the direction of the arrow. Every symbol with a white arrow refers to the second of the four symbols encountered in the direction of the arrow.

Can you complete the original grid?

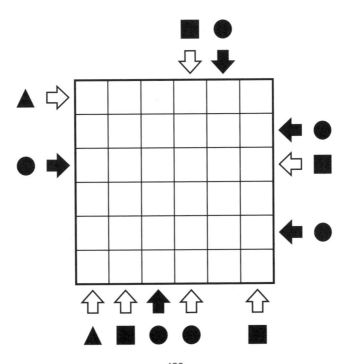

Mind Over Matter

Given that the letters are valued 1-26 according to their places in the alphabet, can you crack the mystery code to reveal the missing letter?

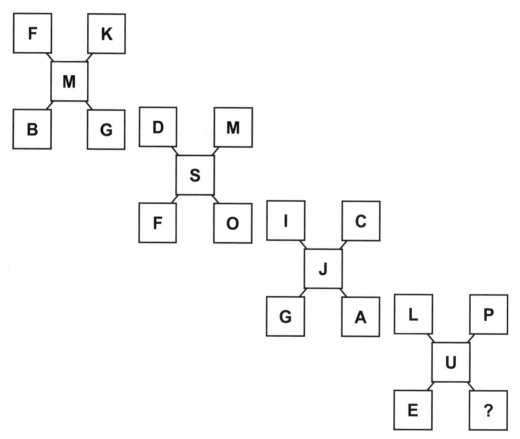

127   Whatever Next?

Which of the four lettered alternatives (A, B, C or D) fits most logically into the empty square?

J	F	M
A	M	J
J	A	S

O	N	D
J	F	M
A	M	J

J	A	S
O	N	D
J	F	M

?

A	M	J
J	A	S
O	N	D

A

F	M	A
M	J	J
A	S	O

B

M	A	J
S	A	J
D	N	O

C

N	D	J
F	M	A
M	J	J

D

128   The Bottom Line

Can you fill each square in the bottom line with the correct digit?

Every square in the solution contains only one digit from each of the lettered lines above, although two or more squares in the solution may contain the same digit.

At the end of every row is a score, which shows:

a the number of digits placed in the correct finishing position on the bottom line, as indicated by a tick; and

b the number of digits which appear on the bottom line, but in a different position, as indicated by a cross.

SCORE

7	1	3	4	✗
3	7	0	2	✓ ✓
5	6	7	4	✗ ✗
5	3	1	0	✓
5	5	1	7	✗
				✓ ✓ ✓ ✓

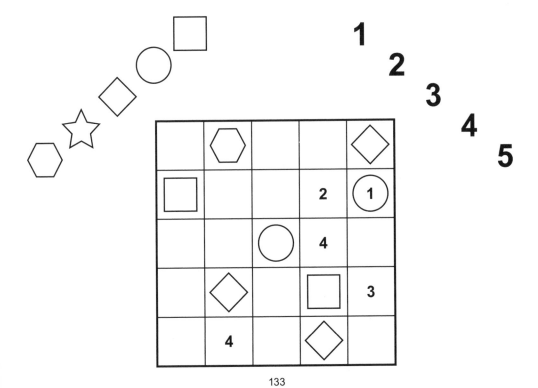

129   **Combiku**

Each horizontal row and vertical column should contain five different shapes and five different numbers.

Every square will contain one number and one shape and no combination may be repeated anywhere else in the puzzle; so, for instance, if a square contains a 3 and a star, then no other square containing a 3 will also contain a star and no other square with a star will contain a 3.

Ls in Place

Twelve L-shapes like the ones here need to be inserted in the grid and each L has one hole in it.

There are three pieces of each of the four kinds shown here and any piece may be turned or flipped over before being put in the grid. No pieces of the same kind may touch, even at a corner.

The pieces fit together so well that you cannot see any spaces between them; only the holes show. Can you tell where the Ls are?

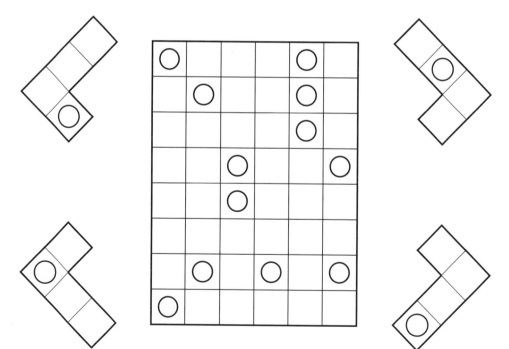

Box Clever

When the box below is folded to form a cube, just one of the five alternatives (A, B, C, D or E) can be produced. Which?

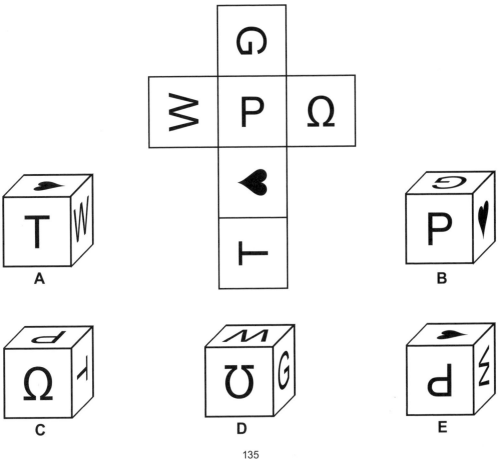

Latin Square

The grid should be filled with numbers from 1 to 6, so that each number appears just once in every row and column. The clues refer to the digit totals in the squares, for example A 1 2 3 = 6 means that the numbers in squares A1, A2 and A3 add up to 6.

1 C 3 4 = 3

2 D 2 3 4 = 12

3 E 1 2 = 3

4 F 4 5 = 8

5 A B 1 = 11

6 A B 2 = 7

7 E F 3 = 10

8 A B 4 = 4

9 D E 5 = 9

10 C D E 6 = 8

11 A 5 6 = 7

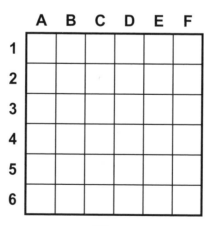

Eliminator

Every oval shape in this diagram contains a different letter of the alphabet from A to K inclusive. Use the clues to determine their locations. Reference in the clues to 'due' means in any location along the same horizontal or vertical line.

1 The A is next to and west of the K, which is due north of both the G and the H.

2 The B is next to and west of the H, which is next to and west of the E.

3 The F is next to and south of the G, which is not next to the I.

4 The C is further west than the I, which is further south than the J, which is further west than the D.

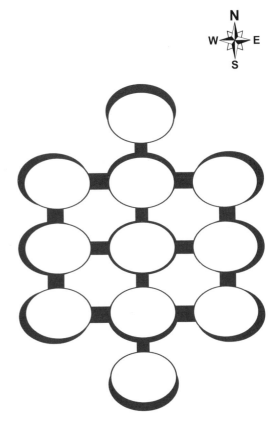

Battleships

Can you place the vessels into the diagram? Some parts of vessels or sea squares have already been filled in. A number to the right or below a row or column refers to the number of occupied squares in that row or column. Any vessel may be positioned horizontally or vertically, but no part of a vessel touches part of any other vessel, either horizontally, vertically or diagonally.

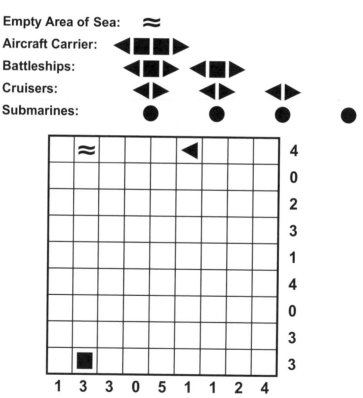

Coin Collecting

In this puzzle, an amateur coin collector has been out with his metal detector, searching for booty. He didn't have time to dig up all the coins he found, so has made a grid map, showing their locations, in the hope that if he loses the map, at least no-one else will understand it... However, he didn't count on YOU coming across the strange grid (as seen here). Will you be able to discover the correct number of coins and their precise locations?

Those squares containing numbers are empty, but where a number appears in a square, it indicates how many coins are located in the squares (up to a maximum of eight) surrounding the numbered one, touching it at any corner or side. There is only one coin in any individual square. Place a circle into every square containing a coin.

	1	1		1		2	1	2	
3				2		1		1	1
			3		1				
		3						0	
2				1			1		
	6		4			1			
3							0		0
	6	5	5	3				1	
				1		1			

Slitherlink

Draw a single continuous loop, by connecting the dots. No line may cross the path of another.

The figure inside each set of any four surrounding dots indicates the total number of surrounding lines.

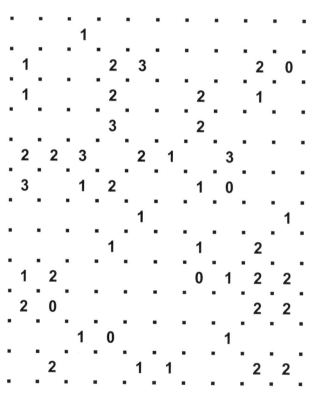

Logi-6

Every row and column of this grid should contain one each of the letters A, B, C, D, E and F.

In addition, each of the six shapes (marked by thicker lines) should also contain one each of the letters A, B, C, D, E and F.

Can you complete the grid?

Piecework

Place all twelve of the pieces into the grid. Any may be rotated or flipped over, but none may touch another, not even diagonally. The numbers outside the grid refer to the number of consecutive black squares; and each block is separated from the others by at least one white square. For instance, '3 2' could refer to a row with none, one or more white squares, then three black squares, then at least one white square, then two more black squares, followed by any number of white squares.

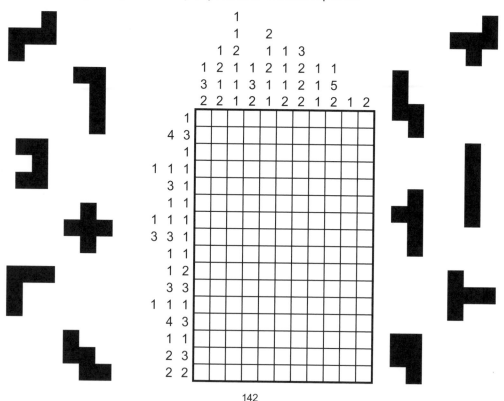

Tile Twister

Place the eight tiles into the puzzle grid so that all adjacent numbers on each tile match up. Tiles may be rotated through 360 degrees, but none may be flipped over.

4	4				
2	3				

2	2
4	1

2	2
4	3

2	4
4	1

3	2
3	1

3	1
3	3

2	2
1	3

3	4
1	3

3	1
4	2

Spot Numbers

The numbers at the top and on the left side show the quantity of single-digit numbers (1-9) used in that row and column. The numbers at the bottom and on the right show the sum of the digits. A number may appear more than once in a row or column, but no numbers are in squares that touch, even at a corner.

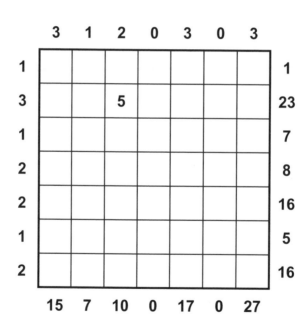

Domino Placement

A standard set of 28 dominoes has been laid out as shown.

Can you draw in the edges of them all? The check-box is provided as an aid, so that you can see which dominoes have been located.

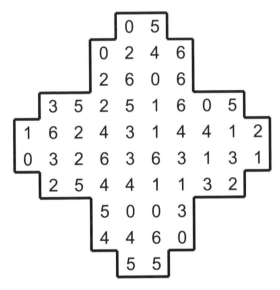

0-0	0-1	0-2	0-3	0-4	0-5	0-6	1-1	1-2	1-3	1-4	1-5	1-6	2-2

2-3	2-4	2-5	2-6	3-3	3-4	3-5	3-6	4-4	4-5	4-6	5-5	5-6	6-6

Hexagony

Can you place the hexagons into the grid, so that where any hexagon touches another along a straight line, the contents of both triangles is the same? No rotation of any hexagon is allowed!

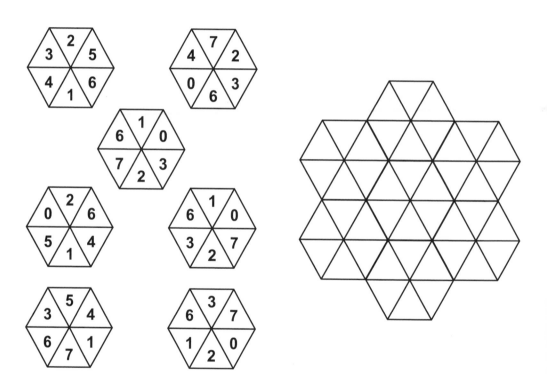

143   Simple as A, B, C?

Each of the small squares in the grid below contains either A, B or C. Every row, column and each of the two long diagonals has exactly two of each letter. The information in the clues refers only to the squares in that row or column. To help you solve this problem, we have provided as many clues as we think you will need! Can you tell the letter in each square?

Across
1 No two adjacent squares contain the same letter.
2 The As are further right than the Bs.
3 The Bs are further right than the As.
4 The Cs are further right than the Bs.
5 Each A is next to and right of a B.
6 No two adjacent squares contain the same letter.

Down
1 The As are somewhere between the Cs.
2 The Bs are lower than the Cs.
3 Any three adjacent squares contain three different letters.
4 The Cs are lower than the Bs.
5 The Cs are somewhere between the Bs.
6 Each B is next to and below an A.

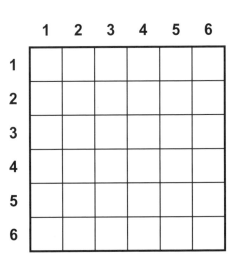

Total Concentration

The blank squares below should be filled with whole numbers between 1 and 40 inclusive, any of which may occur more than once, or not at all.

The numbers in every horizontal row add up to the totals on the right, as do the two long diagonal lines; whilst those in every vertical column add up to the totals along the bottom.

Can you discover the missing numbers?

								171
29		26	20	3	8		25	168
20	1	28	28	36	15			183
	8	26	19	21		12		125
14	27	15	39	15	11		22	171
16	14	27	9			31	17	182
	22		28	38	1	7	10	172
31		25		31	17	32	4	192
7	20	12	12		29		22	143
154	171	194	167	203	120	179	148	183

Shape Up

Every row and column in this grid originally contained one circle, one diamond, one square, one triangle and two blank squares, although not necessarily in that order.

Every symbol with a black arrow refers to the first of the four symbols encountered when travelling in the direction of the arrow. Every symbol with a white arrow refers to the second of the four symbols encountered in the direction of the arrow.

Can you complete the original grid?

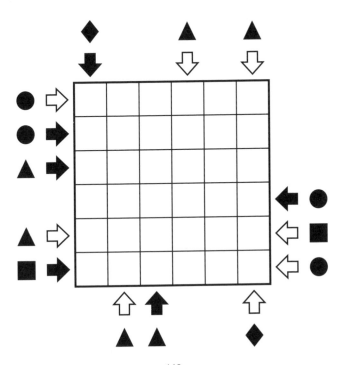

Given that the letters are valued 1-26 according to their places in the alphabet, can you crack the mystery code to reveal the missing letter?

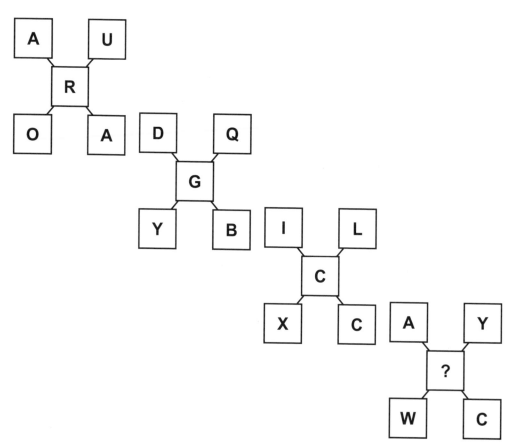

Whatever Next?

Which of the four lettered alternatives (A, B, C or D) fits most logically into the empty square?

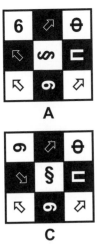

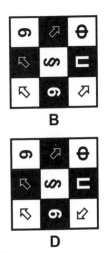

The Bottom Line

Can you fill each square in the bottom line with the correct digit?

Every square in the solution contains only one digit from each of the lettered lines above, although two or more squares in the solution may contain the same digit.

At the end of every row is a score, which shows:

  a the number of digits placed in the correct finishing position on the bottom line, as indicated by a tick; and

  b the number of digits which appear on the bottom line, but in a different position, as indicated by a cross.

SCORE

0	4	0	3	✗
0	2	1	0	✗
5	0	6	4	✓ ✗
2	6	4	5	✗
6	5	7	3	✗ ✗
				✓ ✓ ✓ ✓

149

Combiku

Each horizontal row and vertical column should contain five different shapes and five different numbers.

Every square will contain one number and one shape and no combination may be repeated anywhere else in the puzzle; so, for instance, if a square contains a 3 and a star, then no other square containing a 3 will also contain a star and no other square with a star will contain a 3.

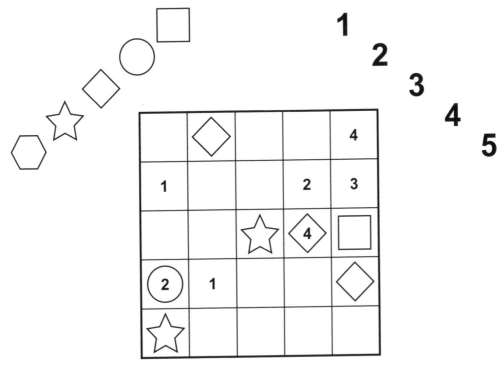

Ls in Place

Twelve L-shapes like the ones here need to be inserted in the grid and each L has one hole in it.

There are three pieces of each of the four kinds shown here and any piece may be turned or flipped over before being put in the grid. No pieces of the same kind may touch, even at a corner.

The pieces fit together so well that you cannot see any spaces between them; only the holes show. Can you tell where the Ls are?

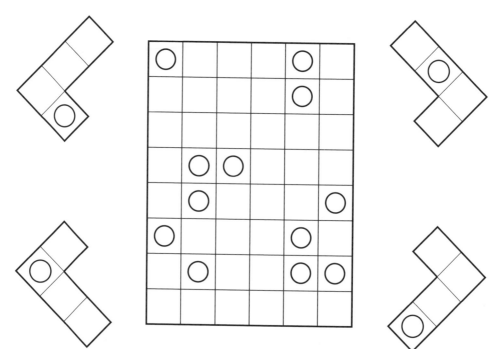

Box Clever

When the box below is folded to form a cube, just one of the five alternatives (A, B, C, D or E) can be produced. Which?

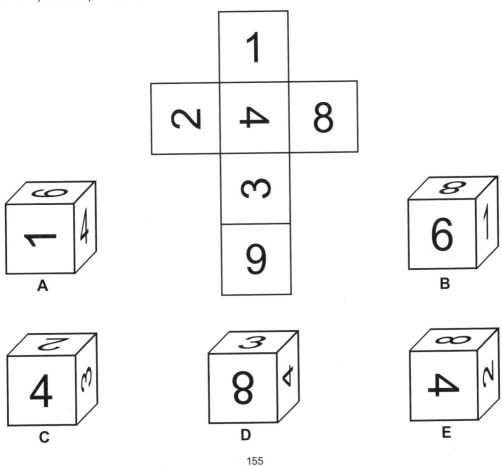

Latin Square

The grid should be filled with numbers from 1 to 6, so that each number appears just once in every row and column. The clues refer to the digit totals in the squares, for example A 1 2 3 = 6 means that the numbers in squares A1, A2 and A3 add up to 6.

1 B C D 5 = 10

2 C D 6 = 3

3 A 4 5 = 3

4 B 1 2 = 10

5 C 2 3 = 10

6 D 1 2 = 11

7 E 3 4 5 = 12

8 F 3 4 = 9

9 E F 1 = 5

10 E F 2 = 3

11 A B 3 = 5

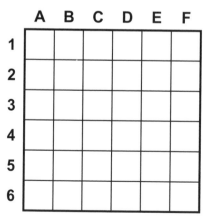

153   Eliminator

Every oval shape in this diagram contains a different letter of the alphabet from A to K inclusive. Use the clues to determine their locations. Reference in the clues to 'due' means in any location along the same horizontal or vertical line.

1 The A is due east of both the C and the J.

2 The B is due east of the I, due west of the H and due north of the G.

3 The C is next to and south of the K, which is next to and west of the D.

4 The E is further south and further east than the F, which is next to the D.

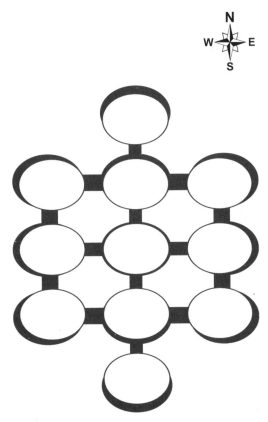

154

Battleships

Can you place the vessels into the diagram? Some parts of vessels or sea squares have already been filled in. A number to the right or below a row or column refers to the number of occupied squares in that row or column. Any vessel may be positioned horizontally or vertically, but no part of a vessel touches part of any other vessel, either horizontally, vertically or diagonally.

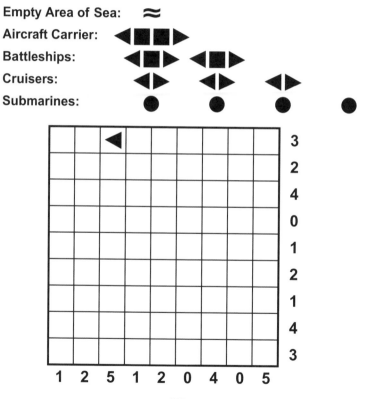

Coin Collecting

In this puzzle, an amateur coin collector has been out with his metal detector, searching for booty. He didn't have time to dig up all the coins he found, so has made a grid map, showing their locations, in the hope that if he loses the map, at least no-one else will understand it... However, he didn't count on YOU coming across the strange grid (as seen here). Will you be able to discover the correct number of coins and their precise locations?

Those squares containing numbers are empty, but where a number appears in a square, it indicates how many coins are located in the squares (up to a maximum of eight) surrounding the numbered one, touching it at any corner or side. There is only one coin in any individual square. Place a circle into every square containing a coin.

		1	1				2	1
0				2			2	
	2			2			1	
0	1	2			3	2		
	2			4				
			2				3	3
0								
	4		2			2	4		4
			2	2				
	2		1			2		2	

Slitherlink

Draw a single continuous loop, by connecting the dots. No line may cross the path of another.

The figure inside each set of any four surrounding dots indicates the total number of surrounding lines.

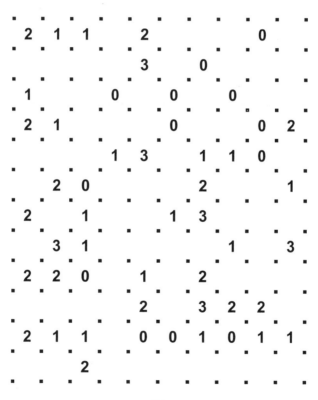

Logi-6

Every row and column of this grid should contain one each of the letters A, B, C, D, E and F.

In addition, each of the six shapes (marked by thicker lines) should also contain one each of the letters A, B, C, D, E and F.

Can you complete the grid?

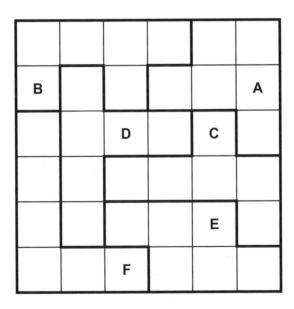

Piecework

Place all twelve of the pieces into the grid. Any may be rotated or flipped over, but none may touch another, not even diagonally. The numbers outside the grid refer to the number of consecutive black squares; and each block is separated from the others by at least one white square. For instance, '3 2' could refer to a row with none, one or more white squares, then three black squares, then at least one white square, then two more black squares, followed by any number of white squares.

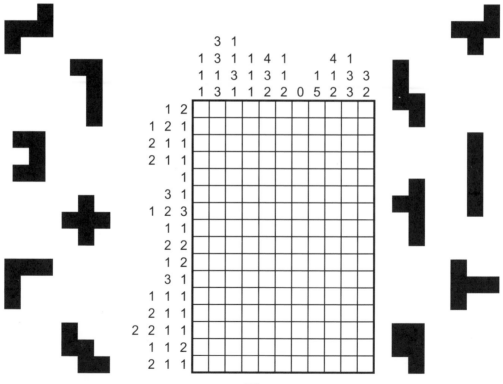

Tile Twister

Place the eight tiles into the puzzle grid so that all adjacent numbers on each tile match up. Tiles may be rotated through 360 degrees, but none may be flipped over.

4	2				
1	1				

4	3
2	4

4	2
1	2

2	2
2	3

1	2
4	3

4	1
2	2

4	3
1	4

4	3
2	2

1	2
2	3

Spot Numbers

The numbers at the top and on the left side show the quantity of single-digit numbers (1-9) used in that row and column. The numbers at the bottom and on the right show the sum of the digits. A number may appear more than once in a row or column, but no numbers are in squares that touch, even at a corner.

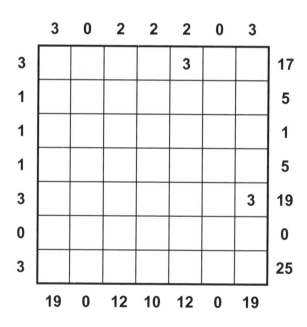

Domino Placement

A standard set of 28 dominoes has been laid out as shown.

Can you draw in the edges of them all? The check-box is provided as an aid, so that you can see which dominoes have been located.

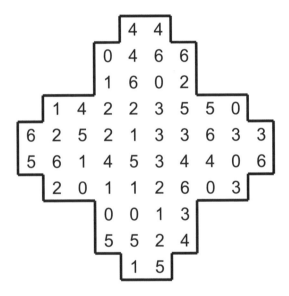

0-0	0-1	0-2	0-3	0-4	0-5	0-6	1-1	1-2	1-3	1-4	1-5	1-6	2-2

2-3	2-4	2-5	2-6	3-3	3-4	3-5	3-6	4-4	4-5	4-6	5-5	5-6	6-6

Hexagony

Can you place the hexagons into the grid, so that where any hexagon touches another along a straight line, the contents of both triangles is the same? No rotation of any hexagon is allowed!

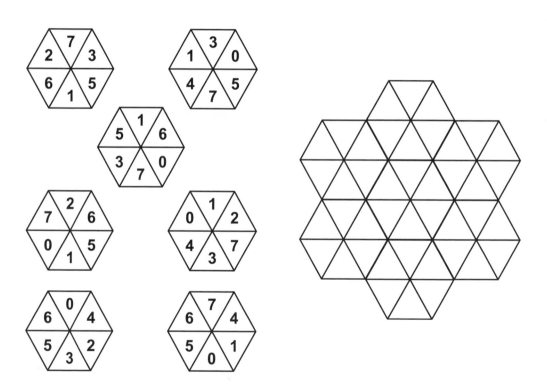

163   **Simple as A, B, C?**

Each of the small squares in the grid below contains either A, B or C. Every row, column and each of the two long diagonals has exactly two of each letter. The information in the clues refers only to the squares in that row or column. To help you solve this problem, we have provided as many clues as we think you will need! Can you tell the letter in each square?

Across

1 Each C is next to and right of a B.

3 No two adjacent squares contain the same letter.

4 Each A is next to and right of a C.

5 No two adjacent squares contain the same letter.

6 The Bs are somewhere between the As.

Down

2 No two adjacent squares contain the same letter.

3 The As are next to one another.

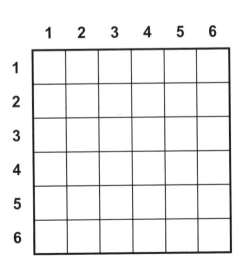

Solutions

1

```
          2 6
        0 0 6 6
        1 2 4 5
    3 5 0 2 5 1 1 4
  1 6 6 4 6 2 6 3 1 3
  0 4 3 5 1 5 5 3 3 2
    2 4 0 3 4 0 1 0
        5 2 2 6
        5 1 3 0
          4 4
```

2

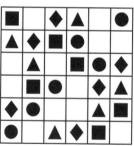

3

A	C	B	A	C	B
B	B	C	A	C	A
A	C	A	B	B	C
C	B	A	C	A	B
B	A	C	C	B	A
C	A	B	B	A	C

4

1	24	33	36	10	9	16	10
39	22	22	2	5	15	16	13
11	7	18	14	8	26	17	24
21	18	14	35	28	9	37	39
5	3	31	38	37	5	21	6
20	4	7	1	5	32	24	34
12	27	18	15	14	1	8	18
32	32	35	14	39	14	20	14

5

(grid of shapes)

6

The value of the letter in the top left square, minus the value of the letter in the bottom right square, equals that of the central square, as does the value of the letter in the top right square, minus the value of the letter in the bottom left square. Thus the missing value is 15, so the missing letter is O.

7

C – Starting in the top right-hand square and moving in the direction of the arrow, the last square becomes the first square of the next sequence each time.

8

2310

Solutions

9

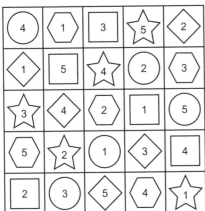

10

11
D

12

3	1	4	5	6	2
6	5	3	2	4	1
2	4	5	6	1	3
5	6	2	1	3	4
4	2	1	3	5	6
1	3	6	4	2	5

13

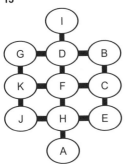

14

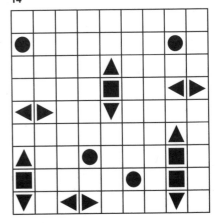

169

Solutions

15

●	3	●	1		●			●	1
2	●			1	2		3	2	1
	1			1		●	●		
1		1	●		1		●	4	1
●	1		2			2	●	4	●
				●		2	4	●	3
	0		●	●	4	●		●	
		2			●		4		3
●	3	●		1		2	●	●	●
1	3	●				1	2	3	

16

2	.	1	1	1		2			.
1				3		2		0	.
		1	1	1		2	3		
	2	2	2			1			
1	3	2				1	3		
	1		2	1	3		0	2	
3		0				1	1		
	1	3				2	3		
1					2	1			
1	0	1		1		2		2	.
2	2		3		2		3	.	1
.	.	.			2				

17

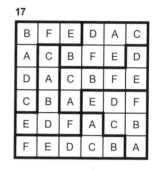

B	F	E	D	A	C
A	C	B	F	E	D
D	A	C	B	F	E
C	B	A	E	D	F
E	D	F	A	C	B
F	E	D	C	B	A

18

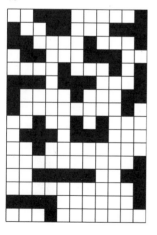

19

1	3	3	4	4	1
3	2	2	4	4	2
3	2	2	4	4	2
2	1	1	2	2	2
2	1	1	2	2	2
3	4	4	2	2	3

20

9		1		6		
2					9	
			5			
9					5	
		1				
5				3		5

Solutions

21

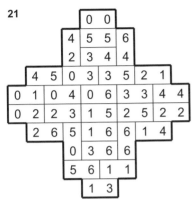

22

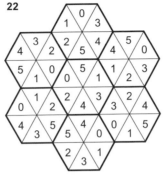

23

B	B	A	C	C	A
A	C	C	B	B	A
A	C	B	B	A	C
B	A	C	A	C	B
C	A	B	C	A	B
C	B	A	A	B	C

24

11	21	29	27	4	12	24	31
13	17	10	1	39	29	36	21
19	9	36	10	8	12	10	15
40	4	9	23	35	40	14	18
33	36	24	34	37	30	24	19
37	32	37	28	1	17	27	9
31	37	16	28	31	16	33	5
19	38	21	3	14	17	7	34

25

26

The sum total of the values of the letters in the top left and bottom left squares equals that of the central square, as does the sum total of the values of the letter in the top right and bottom right squares. Thus the missing value is 24, so the missing letter is X.

27

C – The shape within each of the squares in the left column makes a quarter turn anticlockwise, the shape within each of the squares in the central column makes a half turn and the shape within each of the squares in the right column makes a quarter turn clockwise every time.

28

5574

Solutions

29

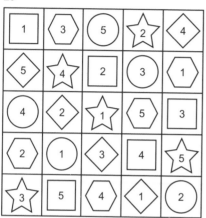

30

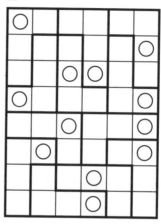

31
B

32

1	3	5	6	4	2
3	2	4	5	6	1
6	4	1	2	5	3
5	1	6	3	2	4
2	6	3	4	1	5
4	5	2	1	3	6

33

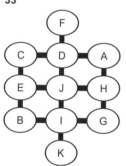

34

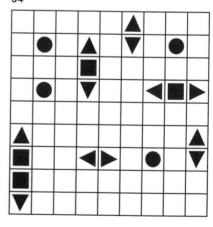

Solutions

35

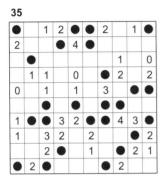

36

37

E	D	F	A	C	B
B	E	A	C	D	F
F	B	D	E	A	C
C	A	B	F	E	D
D	C	E	B	F	A
A	F	C	D	B	E

38

39

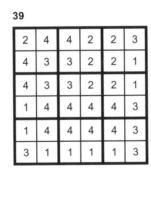

2	4	4	2	2	3
4	3	3	2	2	1
4	3	3	2	2	1
1	4	4	4	4	3
1	4	4	4	4	3
3	1	1	1	1	3

40

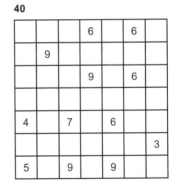

173

Solutions

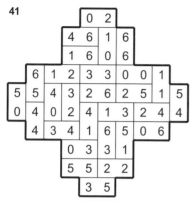

41

			0	2					
		4	6	1	6				
		1	6	0	6				
	6	1	2	3	3	0	0	1	
5	5	4	3	2	6	2	5	1	5
0	4	0	2	4	1	3	2	4	4
	4	3	4	1	6	5	0	6	
		0	3	3	1				
		5	5	2	2				
			3	5					

42

43

C	C	B	B	A	A
A	B	C	A	C	B
B	C	A	B	C	A
A	B	C	A	B	C
C	A	A	C	B	B
B	A	B	C	A	C

44

2	35	17	10	17	40	24	32
6	6	5	37	34	6	23	30
5	7	34	6	25	1	28	6
10	23	8	31	1	14	3	8
34	5	29	7	29	35	38	20
26	23	35	22	14	7	26	25
8	28	36	10	5	9	7	40
22	31	17	24	32	12	30	23

45

46

The sum total of the values of the letters in the top two squares, multiplied by the value of the central letter equals the sum total of the values of the letters in the bottom two squares. Thus the missing value is 23, so the missing letter is W.

47

D – The letters move in the direction of the arrow as shown, with the final letter moving to take the place of the first letter:

48

1051

Solutions

49

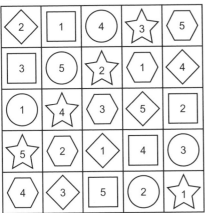

50

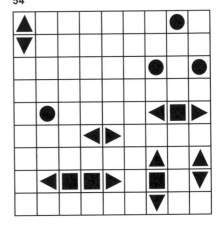

51

A

52

4	1	3	2	6	5
6	5	4	1	3	2
2	4	6	5	1	3
1	3	2	6	5	4
5	2	1	3	4	6
3	6	5	4	2	1

53

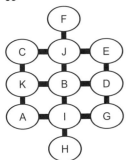

54

175

Solutions

55

2	●	2			●		1	1	1
●	4	●	1	1				●	2
●	4		1		0		2		●
2	●		2					●	
		●	●	1		2		2	
●	4	3				●		1	●
●		●			●	3			1
2					3	●	3		1
●		1		●			●	●	1
2	●		1	2	●	●	3	2	

56

2	1		1			1		3	·
	3	2	1						·
1		1	2	2			3	2	
			2	3		1	0		
1	2	2	2			·	·		1
	0		2	0					
2		3			0	1	1		
1	3		1	0		2		2	
3		1			3		2		
	3		2	3		2		2	
2	1	·		1	1		2		
2		1	·	3		2	2		

57

D	B	A	F	E	C
B	E	D	A	C	F
E	F	B	C	A	D
A	C	E	D	F	B
C	D	F	E	B	A
F	A	C	B	D	E

58

59

4	3	3	3	3	2
1	1	1	2	2	4
1	1	1	2	2	4
3	3	3	2	2	4
3	3	3	2	2	4
4	2	2	1	1	4

60

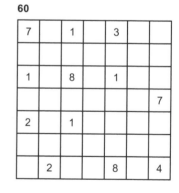

7		1		3		
1		8		1		
						7
2		1				
	2			8		4

176

Solutions

61

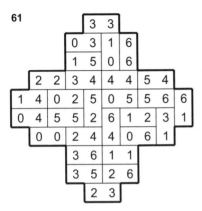

62

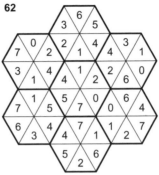

63

C	A	A	B	C	B
C	B	B	C	A	A
B	C	A	C	B	A
A	A	B	B	C	C
B	C	C	A	A	B
A	B	C	A	B	C

64

37	38	7	14	8	3	10	21
13	3	35	40	24	15	37	10
25	17	5	19	16	17	11	11
11	9	11	25	2	15	1	20
32	15	12	21	11	20	18	6
10	33	9	6	18	26	23	25
26	18	2	39	4	12	29	20
4	24	30	20	22	39	28	38

65

66

The sum total of the letters in the top three squares is equal to the sum total of the values of the letters in the bottom two squares. Thus the missing value is 21, so the missing letter is U.

67

B – Each letter makes a quarter turn clockwise every time and the letters move one place forward in the alphabet.

68

5540

Solutions

69

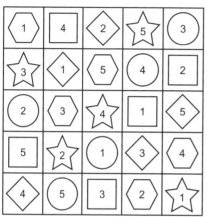

70

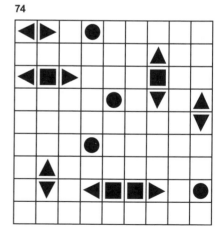

71
E

72

2	3	6	1	4	5
5	2	4	3	1	6
1	6	5	2	3	4
6	4	3	5	2	1
3	5	1	4	6	2
4	1	2	6	5	3

73

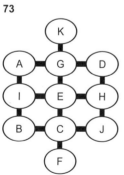

74

178

Solutions

75

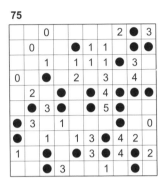

76

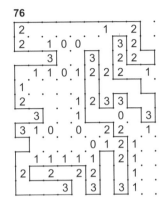

77

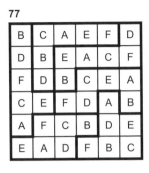

B	C	A	E	F	D
D	B	E	A	C	F
F	D	B	C	E	A
C	E	F	D	A	B
A	F	C	B	D	E
E	A	D	F	B	C

78

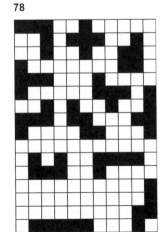

79

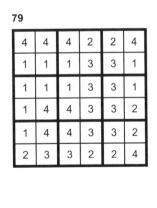

4	4	4	2	2	4
1	1	1	3	3	1
1	1	1	3	3	1
1	4	4	3	3	2
1	4	4	3	3	2
2	3	3	2	2	4

80

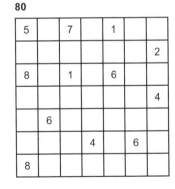

5		7		1		
						2
8		1		6		
						4
	6					
			4		6	
8						

Solutions

81

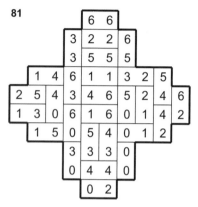

82

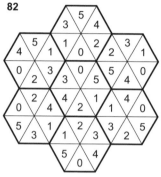

83

A	C	B	C	A	B
B	B	A	C	A	C
B	A	C	A	C	B
A	A	C	B	B	C
C	B	B	A	C	A
C	C	A	B	B	A

84

18	11	18	20	39	37	19	7
19	34	34	14	8	28	5	8
39	31	34	39	5	34	36	25
28	38	7	19	21	1	14	36
39	31	14	36	38	31	34	19
11	29	31	10	5	5	8	39
28	10	14	3	34	2	16	20
19	21	38	1	38	6	38	38

85

86

The sum total of the values of the letters in the top two squares, minus the sum total of the values of the letters in the bottom two squares, equals the value of the central square. Thus the missing value is 23, so the missing letter is W.

87

C – Each square in the central row contains a number which is the sum of the number in the square above plus the number in the square below.

88

2151

Solutions

89

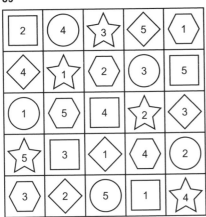

90

91
B

92

2	6	1	5	3	4
6	3	5	2	4	1
3	1	2	4	5	6
1	5	4	6	2	3
4	2	3	1	6	5
5	4	6	3	1	2

93

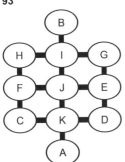

94

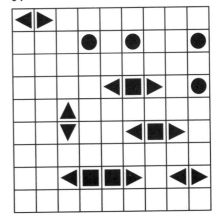

Solutions

95

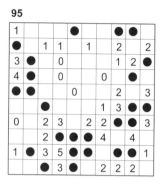

96

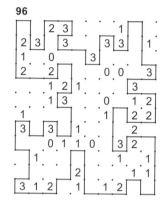

97

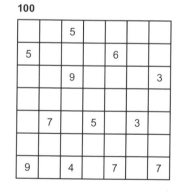

F	C	B	A	E	D
D	F	E	B	A	C
C	D	F	E	B	A
E	A	C	F	D	B
B	E	A	D	C	F
A	B	D	C	F	E

98

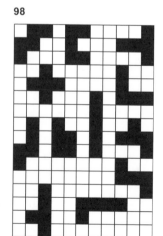

99

1	1	1	3	3	2
2	4	4	4	4	4
2	4	4	4	4	4
3	1	1	2	2	1
3	1	1	2	2	1
4	2	2	1	1	3

100

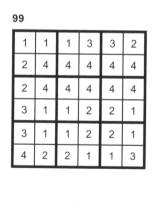

Solutions

101

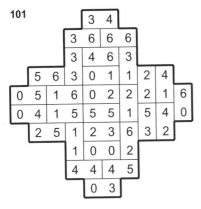

102

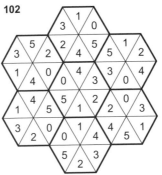

103

B	A	C	C	B	A
A	C	C	B	B	A
A	A	B	C	C	B
B	C	A	A	C	B
C	B	B	A	A	C
C	B	A	B	A	C

104

31	15	38	15	17	7	28	17
22	6	13	38	12	18	34	27
22	2	15	9	14	39	17	17
38	39	8	39	23	30	8	2
10	2	14	23	16	3	1	11
32	8	38	5	12	7	40	5
3	36	11	27	29	37	38	11
35	38	8	35	16	38	35	10

105

106

The value of the letter in the central square is the sum total of the values of the letters in the surrounding squares. Thus the missing value is 20, so the missing letter is T.

107

B – The numbers in every left column total 23, those in each central column total 24 and those in each right column total 25.

108

5704

Solutions

109

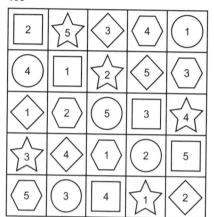

110

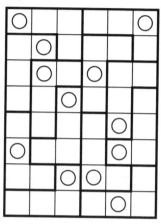

111
C

112

6	1	3	2	4	5
5	6	2	1	3	4
2	5	6	4	1	3
3	2	4	6	5	1
1	4	5	3	6	2
4	3	1	5	2	6

113

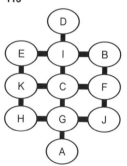

114

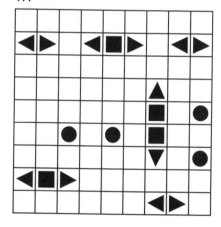

Solutions

115

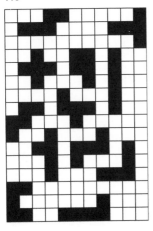

1		●	2		2			●	2
	●				●	●	1		●
		1	1	2	3		3		1
●	1	1				●	●		0
1		3	●	3	●	●			
		●	●	3	3	3	3		
1	●	●		2	2	●		●	1
3	5	●		●		2	3		
●	●		2	2	2		●		
●	3		0		●			1	

116

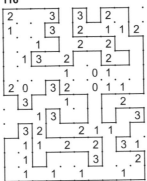

117

F	D	E	B	A	C
D	C	B	E	F	A
A	F	D	C	B	E
C	B	A	F	E	D
E	A	F	D	C	B
B	E	C	A	D	F

118

119

3	1	1	2	2	1
3	2	2	4	4	4
3	2	2	4	4	4
4	1	1	1	1	3
4	1	1	1	1	3
3	1	1	1	1	3

120

		4		7			
9							6
			7				
3						3	
		5					
							2
6		6		9			

Solutions

121

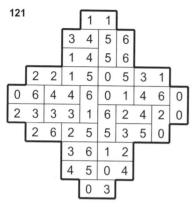

		1	1						
	3	4	5	6					
	1	4	5	6					
2	2	1	5	0	5	3	1		
0	6	4	4	6	0	1	4	6	0
2	3	3	3	1	6	2	4	2	0
	2	6	2	5	5	3	5	0	
		3	6	1	2				
		4	5	0	4				
		0	3						

122

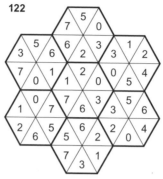

123

B	C	A	C	A	B
B	B	C	C	A	A
A	B	C	A	B	C
C	A	B	A	B	C
A	C	A	B	C	B
C	A	B	B	C	A

124

21	3	24	25	5	38	22	7
3	14	10	30	19	8	12	12
12	7	18	26	18	2	33	24
7	36	29	18	23	37	4	35
15	18	25	2	25	16	6	36
37	14	13	34	32	18	38	34
27	39	3	21	9	34	18	35
14	16	19	19	9	4	21	15

125

126

The sum total of the values of the letters in the top left and bottom right squares equals that of the central letter, as does the sum total of the values of the letters in the top right and bottom left squares. Thus the missing value is 9, so the missing letter is I.

127

A – Read in conventional order (left-right, top to bottom) the letters are the initials of consecutive months of the year, flowing from one large square to the next and with January following December when all twelve have been used.

128

6700

Solutions

129

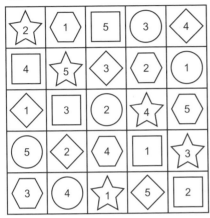

130

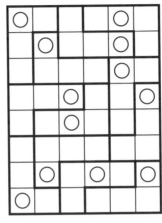

131

E

132

5	6	4	2	1	3
4	3	6	5	2	1
2	5	1	3	6	4
3	1	2	4	5	6
1	4	5	6	3	2
6	2	3	1	4	5

133

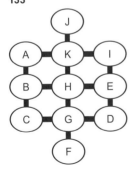

134

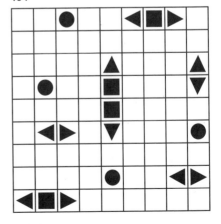

Solutions

135

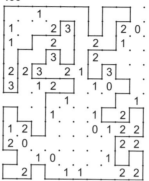

136

137

B	A	D	E	F	C
C	D	B	F	A	E
E	F	C	B	D	A
A	C	E	D	B	F
D	E	F	A	C	B
F	B	A	C	E	D

138

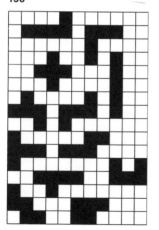

139

4	4	4	3	3	3
2	3	3	1	1	3
2	3	3	1	1	3
2	4	4	2	2	3
2	4	4	2	2	3
4	1	1	2	2	1

140

1						
		5		9		9
7						
		5		3		
7						9
					5	
	7					9

Solutions

141

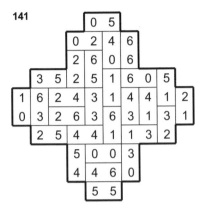

		0	5					
	0	2	4	6			
	2	6	0	6			
3	5	2	5	1	6	0	5
1	6	2	4	3	1	4	4	1	2
0	3	2	6	3	6	3	1	3	1
2	5	4	4	1	1	3	2
	5	0	0	3			
	4	4	6	0			
	5	5					

142

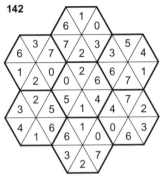

143

C	A	B	A	B	C
B	C	C	B	A	A
A	C	A	B	C	B
A	B	B	A	C	C
B	A	C	C	B	A
C	B	A	C	A	B

144

29	39	26	20	3	8	18	25
20	1	28	28	36	15	36	19
6	8	26	19	21	4	12	29
14	27	15	39	15	11	28	22
16	14	27	9	33	35	31	17
31	22	35	28	38	1	7	10
31	40	25	12	31	17	32	4
7	20	12	12	26	29	15	22

145

146

The sum total of the values of the letters in the top right and bottom left squares, divided by the sum total of the letters in the top left and bottom right squares, equals the value of the central letter. Thus the missing value is 12, the missing letter is L.

147

B – The contents of each black square make a quarter turn clockwise and the contents of each white square make a quarter turn anticlockwise every time.

148

7057

Solutions

149

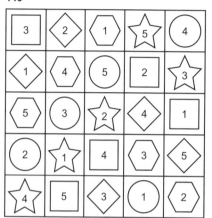

150

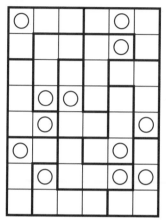

151
D

152

5	4	1	6	3	2
3	6	4	5	2	1
4	1	6	2	5	3
2	5	3	4	1	6
1	2	5	3	6	4
6	3	2	1	4	5

153

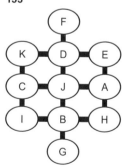

154

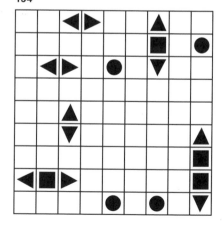

190